GW00602720

Mairéad Byrne
You Have to Laugh: New + Selected Poems

Mairéad Byrne

Mairéad Byrne
You Have to Laugh: New + Selected Poems

Barrow Street Press
New York City

Designed by Robert Drummond
Cover paintings by Michael Cullen
        "Elephant in Blue" (2004, oil on linen, 30 x 40cm)
        "Dancer and Elephant" (2005, oil on linen, 36 x 46cm)

Published by Barrow Street Press
Distributed by:
        Barrow Street Books
        P.O. Box 1558
        Kingston, RI 02881

First Edition

Library of Congress Control Number: 2013933127

ISBN 978-0-9819876-9-9

CONTENTS

State House Calendar (2009)

from *SOS Poetry* (2007)

from *An Educated Heart* (2005)

from *Nelson & the Huruburu Bird* (2003)

from *Tympanum* (work-in-progress)

from *Lucky* (2011)

Notes

Acknowledgments

For Peter Covino

from *The Best of (What's Left of) Heaven* (2010)

ACRES OF COURTESY I WAS PREVIOUSLY UNAWARE OF

[regal wave]: *Be my guest*
[exposed palm, fingers spread]: *Thank you*
[exposed palm, fingers relaxed]: *You're welcome*
[brusque wave]: *Go now minion*
[body of car executing sinuous S-maneuver to allow other driver to cut through backed-up traffic to make a turn, beatific smiles]: *For this millisecond I am your true love forever*

TO MY SURPRISE I FIND MYSELF IN POSSESSION OF THE GLAMOROUS FACTS

The distance from New York City to Boston?
—Approximately 4 hours. By car.

The breeding cycle of periodic cicadas?
—Occurs at prime number intervals of 7, 13, and 17 years.

The "tiles" on the floor in the archway at the entrance to Trinity College, Dublin.
—Are of course blocks: Elizabethan, hexagonal, wooden, and reversible. To counter wear.

—*Quiet.* I know what it is. It is a human hand.

WOULD YOU

So if you could
would you?

Would you—
if you could?

I mean would you—
if you could?

Would you?

Would you really?

Would you—
if you could?

Would you?

WHERE DID YOU GROW UP?

Do you mean why did I grow up?

No—where did you grow up?

Do you mean how did I grow up?

No—*where* did you grow up?

Do you mean when?

No—just where.

Oh!

YOU NEVER KNOW *(formal)*

You never know.
You never know.
You *never* know.
You never *know*.
You never know.

YOU NEVER KNOW *(loose)*

You never know.
You never really know.
You never really know now do you.
You never know.
You just never know.

YOU NEVER KNOW *(wheedling)*

Ah you never know.
Sure you never know do you.
You never really know.
You never never know.
Isn't that the truth.
You never know.

ARE YOU KIDDING ME?

Are YOU kidding me?
Are you KIDDING ME?
Are you kidding me?
Are you kidding me?
ARE you KIDDING me?
Are you *kidding* me?
Are you kidding me?
Are *you* kidding me?
ARE YOU KIDDING ME?

YOU HAVE TO LAUGH

You have to laugh
You have to laugh
Ah you have to laugh
You hafta laugh
You hafta laugh though
Don't you just have to laugh
You hafta laugh
Ah you hafta laugh
You have to laugh
You have to laugh
fuckit

EVERYTHING IS UNLIKELY

Everything is unlikely. Look at going to the bathroom. That's unlikely. And you do it so often. At least four times a day. And sometimes at night too. Sleeping is unlikely. You just conk out. Imagine if you were looking at yourself all those hours. You, hardly daring to breathe, looking at yourself, a great inert heap, hardly breathing, in the dark, and every now & again a gigantic snort. You just get slung down into a pit of sleep. Like those bodies in Pompeii. Then in the morning try to make the pieces flow again. Eating is very unlikely. When it comes down to it—what is it but opening your mouth & putting food in? It's not called a cake-hole for nothing. Mysterious chute. My whole life is unlikely. What is America? Why am I here? What happened to the other country? Where did my sisters' houses go? Why am I here—in this house—in this world—which also holds a man screaming as other men saw at his neck with an inadequate knife?

REALITY IS NOT LIKE ITSELF

Reality is not like itself. My daughter says *I can't believe we have a real live animal in our house!* I think of all the life teeming between floorboards, in heating ducts, under eaves, in the basement, in closets, between folds of comforters and skin. All those perfect systems. The centipede in its skein of dark slung beneath every sliver of brightness in our house. The furry heads of bats under the eaves, asleep during our day and ready to leave, before I even know they are there. The bullish complacence of the dust-mite. Or the long-legged spider in the basement of our house inquiring *Do you believe in an upstairs? I can't believe that there are humans in our house!* And the two of us—in some ways as out of place as the lost fly which stumbles in through the mail-slot, or our lonely cat racing from window to window, aghast & electric, chasing birds, dogs, & feral cats with a house in between—lumbering through rooms scant of everything except books.

A CERTAIN CHARM

Reality has a certain charm. It's really happening. Your breast is being stretched & pulled like dough. It's being flattened between two parts of a machine you're afraid to look at. You'd rather chat to the technician who says *A little more? A little more?* And you say *Okay* until you say *That's enough.* There is no anticipation. It's all now. The light is dim. The temperature is so perfect it's almost slimy. A friendly stranger is manipulating your breast like gum. You inhabit each moment as if it were the base of your very own coconut tree, with your very own pallet & suncream. You are packed into that moment like an embryo in the womb. In the cubicle putting your clothes back on, you might feel ugly. You might feel relieved. You might walk out through the glass doors feeling suave, even cracking a joke. You might sit in your car for a minute thinking *Boy I can drive! I'm gonna drive right back into my life.* And you do, re-entering your living-room like a space capsule splash-down. You exit through the hatch into the stage-set of your home. Small shiny actors run towards you. Nothing seems real. Then sooner or later something really strange happens. Six firemen are standing in huge clothes in your upstairs hallway staring at a beeping alarm. *Now this is real.* It's 3 a.m. It's really happening. A man's large hand reaches out & plucks the carbon monoxide alarm off the wall. You're inhabiting each moment again.

LUDDITE

I'm no Luddite.
I just like saying *Luddite*

EXPECTING THE MAIL

I refuse to accept that this is the mail:
This is not the mail.

I'm looking forward to the mail!

TIP

Here's something I do when I have to get up:
I go back to sleep.

Q & A

Q: Er, guys, could you go a little quieter? It's 5.30 a.m. . . .
A: ARE YOU KIDDING? WE'RE **THE GARBAGE MEN!**

RED SKELETON INTERVIEWS NERVE ENDS, FILAMENTS, & AN ELECTROLYTE

RS: So guys . . .

NFE: **EEEEEEEEEEEEEEEEEEEEEEKKKKKKK!!!!!!!!!**

RS: Hey! That's quite a shriek. Seriously guys . . .

NFE: *ccchhhggggttttcchhhh [abrupt sound made by pushing air forcefully through cheek using reflex propulsive tongue action]*

RS: So you're doing the gig . . .

NFE: *nnnnncccchhhhgggggghhhhkk!!!!!!!!!!*

RS: Huh-huh. Huh-huh. I see where you're going with this . . .

NFE: *EEEeee—EEeeugh—eugh—eugh—eugh—eugh [agonizing creaking / back-of-throat grinding]*

RS: Yeah I see it!

NFE: *SSSKKKRREEEEEEEEEEEENNNNNKKKkkk-k-k-k [hideous chalkboard scraping]*

RS: I kinda see it . . .

RED SKELTON INTERVIEWS JOSEPH THE CARPENTER

Joseph, you were born . . .

—Woe to the day on which I was born into the world! Woe to the womb which bare me! Woe to the bowels which admitted me!

And you were raised by your . . .

—Woe to the breasts which suckled me! Woe to the feet upon which I sat and rested! Woe to the hands which carried me and reared me until I grew up!

I'm sure she did her best . . .

—For I was conceived in iniquity, and in sins did my mother desire me.

Well okay, let's talk about your education . . .

—Woe to my tongue and my lips, which have brought forth and spoken vanity, detraction, falsehood, ignorance, derision, idle tales, craft, and hypocrisy! Woe to mine eyes, which have looked upon scandalous things! Woe to mine ears, which have delighted in the words of slanderers! Woe to my hands, which have seized what did not of right belong to them!

But not your bowels . . .

—Woe to my belly and my bowels, which have lusted after food unlawful to be eaten! Woe to my throat, which like a fire has consumed all that it found!

Joseph, you have based yourself principally in Galilee, traveling a little in Judea and Samaria. Have you ever wished to travel more widely?

—Woe to my feet, which have too often walked in ways displeasing to God! Woe to my body; and woe to my miserable soul, which has already turned aside from God its Maker! What shall I do when I arrive at that place where I must stand before the most righteous Judge, and when He shall call me to account for the works which I have heaped up in my youth?

I don't know Joseph. It's a problem for everyone . . .

—Woe to every man dying in his sins!

That's a bit harsh . . .

—Assuredly that same dreadful hour, which came upon my father Jacob, when his soul was flying forth from his body, is now, behold, near at hand for me.

Surely not!

—Oh! how wretched I am this day, and worthy of lamentation!

Well it's been nice having you on the program Joseph.

—But God alone is the disposer of my soul and body . . .

And so from Red Skelton & Joseph the Carpenter to everyone listening . . .
—He also will deal with them after His own good pleasure!

Goodnight & God bless!

AN INTERVIEW WITH A WISE OLD MAN

MB: You are a wise old man & have lived a long time. Please can you tell me what you have learned?

WOM: Yes.

MB: For example, you have built the house you live in. You use energy powered only from the natural movements of insects in your garden. You have perfected a mineral supplement which, in effect, replaces the necessity for food. You make all your own clothes out of cloth woven by yourself from flax grown in the far field yonder. You have had six wives, each one younger & more beautiful than the one before. All your children have emigrated but send you large packages. Everyone says you are incredibly wise. You have written many books. Today, in what may be the waning years of an incredibly productive life, you seem serene & equanimous. What is the secret of your happiness?

WOM: Happiness.

MB: I see. Very good. You often talk about "chalk," how things must be "chalky," and the essential "chalkiness" of experience. Can you expand on that?

WOM: I was a teacher.

MB: I know. I was your student. They say that everyone should have one great teacher in her. You were mine.

WOM: One feels one's students.

MB: That is so beautiful. You have received many honors in your life. You have won the Pulitzer Prize—twice, gotten four Guggenheims, a MacArthur "Genius" Award, and the Nobel—for both Peace & Literature. These achievements are like some aspiring writer's wet dream. What does it mean to have achieved so much?

WOM: I never got a Pushcart.

MB: Oh, I'm sorry. People say that true happiness is derived from living in the moment, that regardless of what has passed or passing or to come, the thing is to just be in the moment, as fully as possible. To smell the roses & coffee. To be aware of the small hairs rising on the forearm or the back of the neck, the cilia on the caterpillar, the smell of new-baked bread on the window-sill, the taste of a ripe mango, the sound of Bob Marley when his voice breaks or he makes one of those kinda sexual sounds. Is this what it's all about for you? Is this what has caused you to forge a path to wisdom?

WOM: Mm hmm.

MB: That's so great! I feel we're in sync which is weird because I'm not that wise even though I was your student all those years ago and am engaged to you now. But is it ever a strain for you—being a wise old man & having to go out & about wearing wise old man clothes & expressions? Do you ever wish you could just pig out or be unabashedly boorish & selfish like an ordinary old man & give the wisdom a miss for a while?

WOM: Yes.

MB: Oh come here you devil.

EXCERPT FROM AN INTERVIEW WITH CHARLES REZNIKOFF

MB: I read somewhere that you walk 18 miles every day around the city of New York. I read that when your wife, Marie Syrkin, invited you to come along on a trip to Israel you said you couldn't because you hadn't yet finished exploring Central Park. New York doesn't feature at surface level in your work but does its systematic grid, & your steady pacing of it, somehow permeate your work?

CR: I like walking.

MB: Poems are measured in feet; at least the metric foot was at one time the unit of measurement for the poetic line. Is there a sense in which your own poems are measured by the soles of your own feet, laid down again & again on the pavement of New York? On the sidewalks & streets? An invisible routine tracery on the sea-bed of the cacophonous city?

CR: I have my beaten tracks.

MB: Wallace Stevens was in the habit of walking to work at Hartford Accident & Indemnity. He must have been a character about town. People noticed him, & understood he was composing poetry on his walks. There's a story about someone observing Stevens suddenly walking backwards. *He's revising*, the person said. Do you think your own composition is linked to the directionality of your stroll?

CR: My work has a type of carpet-bomb formation. I'm not sure it maps onto the pattern of two feet. Maybe some version is true, e.g., my work is to my feet as New York is to my feet but my work & New York are not at all alike nevertheless.

MB: That's kind of Aristotelian. Let's talk about hands. Do you know *There's the church / And there's the steeple / Open the doors / & there's the people.* Look you can see them wiggling . . .

GREAT BUSINESS IDEAS #9: *TEST-YOUR-POETRY*

**VIGOROUS YOUNG COMPANY PLANTS CHALLENGING
AUDIENCES FOR YOU—
OR YOUR ENEMIES!**

Test **YOUR** poetry on our dedicated audiences of

*NON-ENGLISH SPEAKERS!

*MEN SERVING TIME!

*CHILDREN!

*RICH PEOPLE!

*ENTIRE CLIENTELE OF YOUR LOCAL GYM!

We can arrange for your **VERY SMALL** homogeneous poetry audience to be
REPLACED by a much **LARGER** homogeneous audience in any of our
popular categories!

Audiences can also be clothed in **LIME GREEN, HAIRY WOOL,** or
NUDE, for additional ELECTRIFYING effect.

Imagine your rival's horror when confronted by a sea of **STEWARDESSES**
or **WRESTLERS** in thongs rather than the meager bunch of poetry types
expected!

You can test YOUR OWN POETRY too! Try out new material on
ACROBATS! On RECENT IMMIGRANTS! On THE TERMINALLY ILL!
For a special fee, we can even arrange for an audience of your OWN FAMILY!
Find out if your poetry relates to YOUR OWN FLESH & BLOOD! NO
COUSIN TOO DISTANT TO TRACK DOWN!!!
NO MOTHER TOO SURLY!!!

******SPECIAL******
For a limited time only YOUR reading or your ENEMY'S can be filmed with
WILD CLAPPING by UNIFORMED POLICE* or SENIORS**
as appropriate.

**Only these two groups available for wild clapping momentarily but expansion
plans are in the offing. ** ditto*

AUDIENCE

ENTHUSIASM

I clapped until little drops of blood
jumped out of my finger.

My life is not large-scale—
but intense.

ON CHALKSTONE IN SPRING

Someone lifted up
the very big bowl
of sky
complete with contrails
purple clouds
& scorched
blues

& didn't
quite
set it down
again
letting some
weird atmosphere
& juiced song
leak

into these tiny
streets
even the most
ordinary of
which is slung
under cherry blossom
like quick flame beneath
cupped hands.

GESTURE

A bundled up woman takes a bundled up child by the hand.

A woman bundled up in black holds a child bundled up in colors by the hand.
They walk along Smith Street.

A woman in tight jeans walks away from me. She is holding the hand of a child
in knitted cap & snow boots.

It is snowing. The children walk underneath the snow holding their mothers' hands.

It is Monday, December 4th, the first day of snow. The children are bundled up.
Each child walks to school with their mother, holding her hand.

BLACK MAN STROLLING DOWN HILL MEETS WHITE WOMAN HUFFING UP: STRANGERS

BM: *Hi!* [I am not going to rob you]
WW: *Hi!* [Such a racist thought never entered my head]

A CAR

nosing out
at a funny angle
w/o a driver

is probably just a
car

backing out

from *Talk Poetry* (2007)

CAN YOU DIE OF EATING PANCAKES?

After my hard week's work I decided to make myself a pancake. It was a difficult commitment because I do like my granola. I had to go on a 70-minute drive & take a stiff walk on a breezy beach to brood about it. In the end I decided to put granola *into* the pancake. It was a win-win situation. Happily I set about my task. I remembered a pancake in Olympia Washington once which came with fruit. I cut up a serendipitous half-apple I found in the fridge & threw it in. I was frying this pancake with butter so you can imagine the effect on the apple & how delicious it all smelled. I had to go out of the house (it was cold) & come back in just to truly appreciate the aroma. Ever notice that the only time you *really* get to smell your house's smell is when you come in from outside? I used to think a certain smell was peculiar to Chinese houses until I started coming into my own house after cooking rice. The pancake, when done, was stupendous. It was actually more of a collection of pancakes. It was a pancake in the sense that Providence is a city. Sort of a cluster of pancakelets, each with the integrity & rights of a pancake, of course, especially the right to collect taxes. And no doubt there was one quintessential pancake in there which was the definitive pancake which gave the Providence *gestalt* to the lot of them. Anyhoo (never said that before) it was very high & crumbly. Very complex in its parts. It looked like a lethal weapon—or the results of one. I put lemon on it & maple syrup & set to. I'm still eating it. I'm going to be eating it a very long time. If I die, consider this my 5 lb accidental suicide note.

CHIASMUS

When you marry & divorce your dreams get mixed up. You wanted an over-stuffed leather living room set and next thing you know you're heading an expedition to the South Pole *and* making a pretty good fist of it. There you are on top of the Ross Ice Shelf in the depths of winter hauling supplies to base camp, enduring 25 mph winds and a record low of -64°F with a wind-chill equivalent of -2800°F, watching the sun come up on the horizon for the first time in months when it hits you right between your frost-rimed but piercing eyes: *Wasn't it X's dream to lead an expedition to Antarctica? What am I doing here? How did this happen? How did I inherit his dream?* Meanwhile X is in Cardi's meditating on a handsome cognac top grain leather living room set with dark wood accent trim and dimpled plush back, cushioned and sectioned vertically for style and comfort, wondering if it might perhaps be more pleasing in chocolate or burgundy, harvesting his own ecstasy.

CIRCUS

There's so much emphasis on the individual we forget how much a single person is actually a double. For a start, we are symmetrical: 2 eyes, 2 nostrils, 2 lips with two halves in each one. Our 32 teeth can be divided in two so many ways they deserve a poem of their own. And, taking a bird's eye view—2 hemispheres in the brain. The story goes all the way down: 2 shoulders, 2 arms, 2 lungs, 2 kidneys, 2 testicles, 2 ovaries, 2 bums, each one divided in two, 2 legs, 2 knees, 2 feet. We are actually really 2 people in one. And what do we do? We pair up. We get married, shackled, whatever. Why we do this I do not know. We are already getting quite enough action being 2 people in one but what do you know. We have to have an outside person too, who is also more 2 persons than one. It gets complex. Now you have a 2 X 4. Kids arrive. Each kid adds 2 to the mix. Sometimes there's twins. Pretty soon you have chaos masquerading as a family. I'm thinking of Ben Franklin. Now Ben was the 15th child out of a total of 17 born to his mother. This figure may or may not include 2 children who died. The numbers are staggering. I'm thinking of Mrs. Franklin. This is a woman or, to my way of thinking, practically 2 women, who had 17 or 19 children proceed through her, i.e., 34 or 38, in addition to providing accommodation for the regular visits of Mr. Franklin. This is not a woman. This is a pomegranate. This is the fabled village it takes to raise a child. Mrs. Franklin herself was the green on which the townspeople cavorted. Is it any wonder we thought of *mitosis* and *meiosis* and all that. It's written all over us. How do you end something like this? It never ends.

DEGREES

What happens if you receive someone else's PhD? I'm serious. People always say: *And then I went for my PhD or I got my PhD at Walla-Walla University* but what if you got someone else's by mistake. You wouldn't be able to understand a word of it. It would be so embarrassing. You'd have to say, *And then I got Doug Thomsen's PhD*, or whoever's name was embossed in gold on it. Say it was an MFA! And it still wasn't yours. You'd be stuck saying *And then, aw, then, aw, well then I got this MFA see, I was going for my PhD but I got this, this is what they gave me, it's poetry, prose poetry I think, yaw*. I don't know, there sure are a lot of problems in life. Not least of which is: If you have Tiny Bludgeon's MFA, who the hell has your PhD???? Probably the same motherfucker who has your eyes, your nose, your smile, your ways: THAT CANNIBAL.

DRINKING MY POEM

I was gloomy all through the paella & the paella was beautiful: a vision of shellfish & chicken nestled on succulent rice. It tasted as good as it looked & looked as good as it tasted & there was texture too. You could have worn this paella as an Easter bonnet in Cannes or Antibes or even somewhere singular like Madrid. But I was thinking of racism, of poverty, of American cities & public schools. I tried to talk about it but just got gloomier & made everyone else gloomy too. It was one of those glooms like a shroud: you couldn't see beyond it. I could see a little girl crossing the street by herself. *Gloom.* I could see a small boy walking very slowly to school. *Gloom.* I could hear a teacher screeching & shaming. *On & on & on & on.* I could see the little kids taking it. *Gloom upon gloom.* I could see a bunch of white people at a meeting in a room saying what they want & how they deserve it & how they're going to go about getting it. *Are these my people? Who are my people?* First I was confused & now this inarticulate yet communicable gloom. So I'm gloomy as I pick at nuts & little crunchy things that look like nuts & other crunchy things that look like banana slices. Gloomy through excellent salad with shaved cheese. Gloomy through chocolate mousse surrounded by fat blackberries & sliced strawberries: another vision & explosion of texture & taste. Gloomy when I accept from Lisa's hand—the same hand that laid a dish of shiny black olives on the burnished orange cloth & raised still furled roses around lilies in a tall vase on a low table in the other room—in a fluted green cup, coffee. It is rich, black & very strong. And my gloom is gone.

DUPLICATES

Another fantastic idea is—*duplicates*. It's fine to have one desk lamp say that you carry from room to room. But imagine having a desk lamp on your desk, a desk lamp on your other desk, a desk lamp on your bedside table, and a floor lamp even by the couch. Can you see how incredible that could be? Instead of plugging out the one desk lamp you have and bringing it here & there & up & down the stairs & plugging it in & out you would simply go to wherever you wished to read etcetera and turn the already present lamp on. I have tried this myself at home so I'm not just speaking speculatively. It has revolutionized my life. There's still one glitch in that I put one of the new desk lamps on my daughter's desk. My daughter is at college. Meanwhile I'm soldiering on with my old bedside lamp which has to be plugged in & out because the on/off switch is broken. I decided to borrow my daughter's desk lamp when she was away. The first time I used it I couldn't believe it! There I was bending down to plug in the sucker as usual when it hit me: *Not necessary!!!!!* Now whenever I hear she's coming home I just swiftly switch lamps. In a sense it's almost as if the lamp has been standing quietly on her desk all the time, waiting for the touch of her white hand. There's something very restful about that.

EMISSARY

After 11 years an emissary came from my country. *We missed you* he said. After all these years. He spoke about how things had changed: The embargo was lifted. All the figures were up: Employment, wages, life expectancy. Elections were being held. We met in the library, the largest room in my house. As he spoke I paced back & forth. Recalling those high hard days. Then 11 years. So many others had gone longer with no word, no call. For some, there was no more country. They had gone. They had ceased to exist for their country. Their country ceased to exist for them perhaps. And then one day ceased to exist at all, for anyone. I wondered what he wanted. What was the purpose of his visit, so to speak. He spoke about investment, education, a democratic reconciliation of differences. If I were a fiction writer I could take it from there. I could give you an explanation, a plot, a narrative. But I am a poet. I looked at his hands holding the glass, the intense black of the trim on his coat. I listened to his voice crumbling into dusk & thought about what it was like.

I CAST MY VOTE

I don't have a carriage & it's not Sunday but I ride up the hill in my Sunday best.

I don't have a boat & Carleton Street is not water but I sail up the street.

It is evening. I am exhausted with that true American exhaustion.

I sail to the Fire Station to cast my vote.

The representative outside is like representatives everywhere. He's the one in the warm coat.

Inside the Fire Station it is practically hairy. There are practically puddles on the floor. A woman at a table shouts out to me to close the door.

It is my first time to vote.

Back outside, the representative stretches towards me only vaguely, and only with a murmur and not fingers. But I have all my pride about me like a warm coat.

When we get home, my daughter looks at pictures of polling booths in the literature and says: *We should have gone to one like that! A shiny one.*

We don't have freedom, I told her earlier, *we have freerdom.*

I WENT TO THE DOCTOR

I went to the doctor. It had been so long since I'd seen a doctor I thought she was trying to interview me. When we first met, she said: *Married, Single, Widowed, Divorced?* I thought that was a bit much. But I told her about my children, my husbands, my job, my furnace, my fall. About how I slept like a top. And Gold's Gym. And the sunken garden in the Pendleton House which is a house inside a museum. And my famous story of how I immigrated 11 years ago with $400 and a 7-year-old child. We talked about poetry. Well, duh. But it was actually much broader than most poetry interviews, looser yet more intense. She asked me about drug use. *Marijuana? Cocaine?* That made me laugh. Everyone was so interested in me. It was marvelous. Even the nurse in Reception asked as she was passing: *Do you happen to know your height?* Boy did I! Then the Office Manager arranged all my appointments. I haven't had so much attention since the MLA or my first wedding. I'm going back.

I WENT TO THE GYM

I went to the gym Wednesday. It was a lot of fun. On the treadmill I couldn't help thinking of Oscar Wilde. I'd never been to a gym before. You have to laugh: all of us there putting in a lot of effort and going nowhere. Gym clothes are great. Just by putting them on you get slimmer, tougher, more resilient, more *salmon-like*. They act like some sort of massage. I guess the fabric has a built-in toner. More like a fan belt than clothes. I haven't been to the gym for almost a week but I feel great. Now when I go out I put on my gym clothes. It's not just a matter of sidling down to Walgreens to get something. Or strolling around in flip-flops. Now I have gym shoes & gym shirts & gym pants (not gym shorts though, I know my limits). When I go out I can't help springing up on people's lawns & doing maneuvers & feints & dancing in place. I can't help bopping around. Flip-flops keep you grounded and that's good, that's humble. But gym shoes send you hurtling out into the world like a coiled spring like blistering latex. It's an adjustment for sure, quite the identity change.

WE WENT TO THE MOON

We went to the Moon. We wore puffy suits & boots. We had a lunar module. We collected Moon rock. We bounced around. Later we had a roving vehicle.

Some people said it was a set-up. That it was done in a TV studio. That there should have been stars & the flag moved.

It was a long time ago now, forty years. We went back a few times but then we stopped. There was no atmosphere. The sky was black. Everything was there but it wasn't much.

When I saw the pale sketch of the Moon in the sky this morning I remembered we went to the Moon. Probably.

METAPHOR RECOIL

A hunter examines a block of text. It is nothing like a poem. Though there are similarities. And differences. It is nothing like an elephant. Or a raccoon. Though certainly there are similarities. And differences. The hunter looks squarely at the text & thinks: *Now where can I get me a square cauldron to boil up some chow?* In the wake of that question comes a silence, a whoosh of wind, a rustle of leaves, a sudden darkening of the sky. The hunter is also a poet—and is afraid.

PERSONAL INSURANCE

These are unpredictable times. I got a call from a man at dinner-time who wanted to sell me home security. I was not polite to him. He started to talk about murder. He said, *I know where you live*. It got me thinking. I've seen movies about guys like this. I feel I'm prepared. I take care to keep a fresh copy of myself in my closet at all times. I back up my files. If anything happens to me there will be another Mairéad to look after my children. That's the least I can do. I just can't believe some parents. They don't seem to realize the consequences of sudden death on a family. I mean, you could lose your house. The children would have nowhere to live. They would be split up. Everything would change, even the cat. And what do you do with a little black cat in the event of the death of the mortgage-holder? Send a piece of the cat here, a piece there? No matter which way you look at it, the cat would lose out, or at the very least go through a difficult period of adjustment. And I know all about them. I'm a single parent. I have to think about these things. My dream is to have a whole rack of Mairéads back to back in my closet. Some people might say it's extravagant but I see it as an investment. What can you do when you have children. It's about peace of mind.

REVISION

The dogs in my neighbors' backyard have no way to process misery. We do. The dogs, stretched out in the dusty yard, might feel the sun steal along their broad pelts, slipping like quicksilver between the radiant hairs, & if sufficient pleasure is packed, might even, who knows, heave to their feet, swaying in hazy dance. But whatever about delight, I don't know that they can use pain for anything other than what my neighbors intend, i.e., attack. They do not think: *I will make something of this endless experience of lovelessness, confinement, & exposure to the elements. I will write a crown of sonnets.* Or *We will sing a duet.* But yet, when these streets are rocked by sirens, as they daily are. When children shudder in their coops. When ambulances, those great can openers of noise, slice up our street, I hear the dogs next door—or one of them—come to the chain-link fence & howl in mimicry, matching the siren's wail with fleshy tongue & throat & vocal chords, laying an answering salve, or question, over chaos.

ROSE-COLORED SPECTACLES

Every now and then I check in my rose-colored spectacles to test the rougher selvedges of life. Yesterday I went for a walk a little out of my neighborhood. I was scared. A very mean-faced white pimp pulled his car across the sidewalk in front of me. He wanted to talk but I kept going. Something about his demeanor suggested rabid dog. There was a power outage when I got home. Back out on my street I could hear the tortured screams of a child, high, recurrent, the same frantic notes played over and over. After the lights went back on there was a powerful smell of skunk. Whole neighborhoods crumble when I take off my spectacles. My own face crumbles, the kitchen floor, memory. Small clear patches loom out of the fog. Reality can be the closest imaginable thing to *delirium tremens*. Come to think of it, another name for *rose-colored spectacles* is *car*.

SHINGLE

The shingles on my house are grey & very like a whale except perhaps in
that each one is small & flat rather than huge & relatively round. My
house in general is more like a whale being huge & the sky around being
quite like the ocean except in that it is not wet. Yet the motion &
profundity of the ocean are somehow echoed in the stillness & distance of
the sky. It is water-color rather than water & the clouds move across it like
whales, carrying their houses on their backs.

STATE PATHOLOGIST

I think she had rings. A black lacy bodice. Her bare arms round & small. Pale freckled skin suggestive of red hair. Though her hair is blonde, her expression intent. Her left hand, cool & precise, turning over the chocolate brown slabs of flesh, lifting its folds, her right hand taking notes. This is a woman's body, animated by expertise. The man, in his dying throes, is pinned by the surrounding crowd. He feels their hot pressure, their hunger for his life. They are winding it out of him on their spindles. He drowns in his own breath, his panting opening a tunnel through them. He sees the watery bog, golden reeds, whipped cotton, tattoo of tiny blue flowers, the massive overwhelming sky. Sluices his last draught of pain & is resurrected—2,500 years later— into her hands.

THAT *WEST END BLUES* SYNDROME

What is that *West End Blues* syndrome? You know, when someone says *Ooh West End Blues ooh* & wags their head in disbelief at a total loss for words. *Oooh West End Blues* & then just—aposiopesis. What makes *West End Blues* something that say *Beau Koo Jack* is not? You don't hear people saying *Oooh that Beau Koo Jack*. And *Beau Koo Jack* is a pretty good tune with wild bits. So what is it? What makes *West End Blues* magnificent? It's not that I don't recognize the syndrome. Like you write thousands of "poems" & suddenly— *jackpot!* You got a classic. You recognize it instantly or certainly within a few years & others recognize it too just as quick. You're absolutely thrilled to have produced a classic & don't know how you did it & but *you did it you did it you did it Hallelujah Lord!* But how does the classic thing happen? Why this & not that? Why then & not now? Why him & not me? What gives that *West End Blues* a free march into your soul? So yes you have that opening horn carving a staircase in the sky. Then the slow jog oh yes with the comfy undertow & the cornucopia of promises above & the tease of horn & lulling swing & knocking of the little clappers like Rudolph clip-clopping on the first day of summer. It's quite a stroll. Then some slight complaining from the trombone, some insinuation & suggestion, well isn't that just the way. Then that musy clarinet & Louis's sympathetic *wad-wad-wa wad-wad-wadda*. With the piano marking time oh yes no argument. Then enter Earl for sure with featherlight fingering. Tinkle & thump & trill. The delicious stir-up of it all presided over by that long slow horn arching out & out & out & out. Louis ever so delicate inserting himself to string his tightrope between skyscrapers & pick his way across into the desultory dissolution of the small hours, well it has to happen the dawn. Then Zutty's woodblock click. Oh yes that's something. But what? That is my point here people. And *hey* fyi did you ever wonder what the W.E.B. in Du Bois stood for? You got it.

THE RUSSIAN WEEK

Inside this week is another week & inside that week is another week & inside that week is another week & inside that week is another week & inside that week is another week & inside that week is another week so that instead of 7 days each week is actually composed of 7 weeks each one a little smaller than its container week but still workable & with rosy cheeks. This arrangement is necessary. If a week were only a week *aka* a standard 7-day week it would not be possible to get things done. Therefore *voilà:* The Russian Week. As soon as it becomes apparent that everything cannot get done in the albeit larger, more commodious week, one can simply crack open the inside week, only slightly less commodious in size. Then, when things pile up as they are wont to do, one proceeds to the inside-inside week, its size only slightly less commodious again. And so it goes. I will not go through the process in tedious detail. For that it would be necessary to have an inside-inside-inside-inside-inside- inside-inside week, i.e., 8 weeks in all and obviously that is impossible. There may be some future in developing a system whereby each of the 7 weeks which constitute the week would in turn contain 7 weeks, giving 49 weeks in all inside one week, and indeed the prospect of an *ad infinitum* progression. But this proposal lacks the calm symmetry of the established model. It is knobby & hectic where the other is smooth, rounded, generous, economical—and natural. Thank God for The Russian Week.

THE TIRED TERRORIST

The terrorist was tired. *Goddammit* he said, *I could do with some bacon &
eggs.* He was sick to the back teeth of killing. It was ugly. He'd had
enough. He laid down his shotgun, his nail-bomb, his knife. He emptied
his pockets. He unzipped his jacket. He thought of the spare room in his
mother's house. What he wouldn't give to be under the peach coverlet
right now, morning radio barely audible, shouts of the children outside,
the smell of bacon wafting up the stairs. Or more foreign breakfasts.
Croissants & apricot jam. Fresh bread & honey. Watermelon. Yogurt.
Smoked horse. Even noodles.

THE WIND THAT SHAKES THE BARLEY

My mother sits inside me like a frog. We are watching a movie. It is *The Wind That Shakes the Barley*. At first I think my mother will like it but then I realize she will not. It is dark in the cinema, so dark it seems empty. I am crouched down in my seat & my mother is crouched down in me. On the screen terrible things are happening. Micheál is battered to a pulp for saying his name in Irish. His vitals are smeared across him. The Black & Tans jump their rifle butts into men's faces breaking their noses & teeth. They are panic turned lethal. An octopus of shout. They hack off a girl's hair taking great swipes of her scalp. The Black & Tan captain draws Teddy's fingernails out with a rusty pliers. The Black & Tans kill the boys. The boys kill the Black & Tans. Then the boys kill each other. *The old story we all know we know it so well.* Though it is not spoken about. It is like heavy metals in our bones. We are made of its secrets. My mother is stirring inside me, anxious to eat.

THREE IRISH POETS

Editors of anthologies & special features on Irish poetry take note: I am available for inclusion in such publications in 3 guises: Irish Woman Poet, Innovative Irish Poet and, as the field is currently wide open, Ireland's First Concrete Poet.* I can furnish a complete set of poems for each identity, in addition to sensitively selected yet pronounceable names: Minnie O'Donnell, Irish Woman Poet; Clare Macken, Innovative Irish Poet; and Bo Doyle-Hund, Ireland's First Concrete Poet. Sample available sets include: "My Transistor Radio," "Léim an Bhradáin," "Rites of Passage" (Minnie O'Donnell); "Trans/is/t," "Apostrophe for Finnegan," "Electoral Capacity" (Clare Macken); and "ciúnas," "'," and "18" (Bo Doyle-Hund). I am working on a fourth identity—"A Remarkable Poet in Her Own Right." The tentative title for this character is: "Mairéad Byrne."

*No further jokes about building sites please.

WE HAD A LAUGH

It was at Thanksgiving. We were watching a movie called *The Lake House*. Sandra Bullock went into a bar & ordered a drink. The barman plopped it down in front of her. My daughter said *What did she order?* I said *A glass of milk*. We nearly died laughing at that. At least I did. I don't know what condition my daughter was in. I couldn't see. My eyes were sealed shut. It was all dark. I felt very tight inside. I could feel the seams of my eyelids like a ridge. Laughs were chocking out of me like I was a Pez dispenser. My lips were stretched wide in a rictus—not like a *gape* or anything loose but like a bird's beak. My whole face was turning into a skull. I was laughing. I was happy. But it was kind of disturbing too. I wouldn't want anyone to see me laughing like that. I hoped my daughter was rolling around in her own pandemonium. Though a few weeks ago a fit of laughter overtook me in Thayer Street. I was falling against walls & lurching into stores until my daughter plucked me back by the nape. Anyway at Thanksgiving we had a laugh. Another funny bit was when Sandra Bullock's fiancé was sitting at a desk in the other room behind a giant laptop. I said *Whoa look at the size of his laptop*. Then my daughter said *It's not a laptop. It's a desktop*. That laugh became a great dark sack of its own too. I should get out more.

WHAT IS A CELL PHONE?

A cell phone is a kind of clock. You don't use it to check the time. Though of course you can. You use it to check that you exist. On the porch—*Am I still here?* In the driveway—*Am I here?* In the car—*What about now, am I here?* At the intersection—*Oh golly strangers everywhere buses trucks Mama I'm turning keep talking for God's sake* yeah. You pat yourself down more efficiently than any arresting cop.

A cell phone is a mobile bed. A security blanket. Saran Wrap for the Reichstag of your head.

Cell phones are a new dimension. They have revolutionized the concepts of out & in. You're never really out. Unless you're comatose. And when you're in, you're often out. You can be in your car, perched on your honey's knee, virtually. Or sullen on your couch, staring at your buzzing phone. Are you "in" or "out"? Impossible to tell. A cell phone offers many inexplicables, always in quotation marks.

A cell phone is a motor. You plug your loaf in & before you know it you have exchanged one set of familiar surroundings for another. A cell phone is a stun gun of the *in between* while simultaneously allowing no other state.

State House Calendar (2009)

STATE HOUSE, SEPTEMBER

candle flame against turquoise
pearl against lavender
mint against rose
breast milk on mauve
metal against mackerel
yellowed lace on watered silk
graphite on glass
silhouette on pale blue
eggshell on streaked blue
grey cut-out against sky-blue
velcro on azure
cupped flame on indigo
old snow on cerulean
gravestone on cobalt
sepulchre white against Ascension Day cloud
mausoleum white against Renaissance cloud
light slate against milky cloud
soft white on white
dove grey against white
old bone against smoke
thumbprint in smoke
dead bone on dirty wool
haze on fog
lemon pith on light grey
ivory on blue-grey
rosé against blue-grey
spooky grey on grey
graphite on glass
mauve against ash
shadow on shade

STATE HOUSE, OCTOBER

soft chalk against sheer blue
gazebo against cloud terrace
apricot kernel beneath soaked sky
lemon-tea stain against cracked cup
[knuckle against wool]
smegma against lint
shaving against mucilage
stale oatmeal against gruel
soap against spray
spray against smoke
beacon against cartoon sky
buttercup under soft chin
conch against inky sea
coral against purple glaze
[pink against purple]
[rose against dove]
[rose against stilly light]
[something luminous against something radiant]
diffusion against saturation
stolidity against fluff
pallor against nausea
ache against unease
pain against tumult
[impassivity in the face of failure]
endurance against onslaught
acceptance against judgment
[weariness against perturbation]
gesture against readiness
statement against trauma
vapor against steam
hiccup against grand plan

STATE HOUSE, NOVEMBER

blur against haze
slate against glaze
[fuzz against gauze]
calm against calm
ash against cloud
milk against cup
[palm against brow]
bone against flux
wet newsprint on flock
web against sheen
hemp against smoke
lit paper about to explode
thumbnail against lens
smudge against lens
lens against cloud downsweep
faint green on cloud tumble
grass stain against apricot
stance against drift
incipience against skepticism
biscuit against cornflower
powdered stone against metal
ink surge in tumbler
pale gold against inky cloud
[pallor against slab]
pallor against oblivion
back against wall
something against nothing
vertical against horizontal
fingertip against nape
touch against skin

STATE HOUSE, DECEMBER

dead tooth against factory smoke
grey shade on striated blue
white on grey
sleet against ice
haze on fog
[cupped votive lamp against soft slate]
[cupped votive lamp against ink]
nougat against light sky with cloud puffs
[pineapple on chiffon]
[pith against gauze]
[tallow on gauze]
shade against light
smoke against smoke
verdigris against fog
[lit skull on wet ink]
worn dime against storm clouds
[sky blue behind ivory]
slate against chiffon
[chalk against gauze]
thumbprint on cold paper
light grey on pale blue
almond on milk
hatching on watered silk
deep shadow against dense steam
shale against smoke
orange pith against dove grey
pineapple on pearl grey
shop bread in gruel
tallow against fleece
still grey against scumbled grey
mauve on tangerine tint

STATE HOUSE, JANUARY

cupped palm over white flame against navy sky
chimney stack smoke behind old enamel
lilac against battleship grey
green-grey against soft grey
marshmallow against mauve tint
tangerine tint against steam
whipped cream against tangerine
dove grey on sky blue banded with rose cloud
chalk against clear white banded with purple cloud
mink on mist
frost against down
fog on fog
[cloud in fog]
one cold thing against another
alabaster against snow field
peppermint against cement
cement against pulp
grey velour on white enamel
bone against grey-blue
salted concrete against rose & grey
shell on thin blue
faint yellow against pale blue
[urine on snow]
sweat stain against collar
nicotine against fluff
scissored edge against drained blue
loaded grey against washed turquoise
shadow against fugitive blue
[smoke against turquoise]
charcoal against pale blue
silhouette on milky glass

STATE HOUSE, FEBRUARY

dense appliqué on transparent blue
[wedding cake on sheer blue]
[stark white against blue psych]
[rose against faded blue]
grey-blue against incandescent white
[marble with sky blue & cloud-scarf]
khaki against suffused grey
soft blue against blue veil & rose sash
beaten egg-white against blue ice
blueberry in milk
[jade against peach]
flame against chiffon
cobalt against apricot fuzz
[yellowed page against rose]
ochre on cloud-banded blue
dirty chalk into cloud
[alabaster against radiant blue]
soft marble against mauve cloud
amber against cobalt
[lemon against flame]
[white gold against sky blue]
loaded shadow on blue swell
river ice on light grey
[soft white against soft grey]
impasto on frothy grey
[mink on lint]
[iced almond on smoked glass]
locked grey against Guinness foam

STATE HOUSE, MARCH

sand on smoke
soft lead against streaming & tossed cloud
[mint against cloudy cloud]
putty against pale wash
sable against sky blue
fine wool against silk
stained cotton on snow
felt against fleece
bronze on steel
foam against spray
[margarine against haze]
[margarine against dishwater]
swept grey on pale blue
eye-white against purple-bitten cloud
airforce blue against pale blue
hatching on glass
ash on denim
card against cloud
clipped shadow on glass
buttercream against steam
cocoa butter against mesh
[lemon ice against dishwater]
burnt umber against blue glass
bone against bruised vein
eraser on smudge
cotton swab on grime
[beige on beige]
stone against violet
dust on enamel
shell against bleached blue
[new flame against massy blue]

STATE HOUSE, APRIL

brushed grey against tumbled grey
anonymous grey against palest grey
smoky grey against pale glass
blue haze against grey
[blue mesh against pale grey]
[blue mesh against light grey]
[blue mesh against white-grey]
[blue smoke against smoke]
cream feather against hopeless grey
blue-white against blue-grey
[milk-blue against silver-grey]
powder blue against memory of blue
startling blue against mauve cloud
[wild cotton against rose-grey]
butter against rose
faint rose against palest blue
[palest blue with rose tint]
[light yellow against suffused grey]
saffron against scumbled cloud
cascading yellow against plunging cloud
marble against fog
sable against fur
fuzz on mist
green-grey against steam
dove grey against milky cloud
[cobweb against metallic cloud]
[leaning tower beneath glowering cloud]
cucumber slice against Himalayan peak
mirage against milky screen
brushmark on watered silk

STATE HOUSE, MAY

yellowed grey against poured grey
sedate grey against white computer screen
brushed grey against scrambled light
[marshmallow against cream soda]
lard against fleece
[soap against suds]
tea stain against dirty suds
tea stain against snow
nylon stocking against grimy swab
brushed shadow on porcelain
shadow on dust bowl
blue shadow on glass
[settled dust against open window]
fist against threat
[indifference against threat]
[flinch against threat]
[candy in the palm of a child about to cry]
[forbearance against despair]
[moon against electric cloud]
[bone against cloud]
splintered tooth against racked cloud
[beacon against storm clouds]
ermine against snow
ermine against fuzz
fur against cotton
mink in fog
white smoke against smoke
[bared belly against rumpled comforter]
feather against metal
church candle against cloudy ink
sandwich in church buffet

STATE HOUSE, JUNE

brushstroke against stipple
mothwing against paint
[despair against nonchalance]
blur against comprehension
blur on haze
sigh against pillow
wrinkled bedsheet on cloud hammock
skein against wool
old silver against glass pane
chamois against old iron
chipped cup among cloud suds
vanilla ice against perfect blue
polished white against smoky blue
soft blue against pale sky
soft flame against apricot froth
incandescence against varicose blue
bluish white against old rose
dove breast against blue veil
glance against equanimity
ash against white ash
dust on milk
chalk smear on grey screen
grey breast against blue sky
beacon against purple swathe
pearl drop on bruised mantle
yellow cream against fog
[yellow cream against spray]
[sobriety against morning]
[blessing against finality]
[old head on stark pillow]

STATE HOUSE, JULY

shining white on pearl grey
turquoise against hazy blue
blue ash against clear blue
soft chalk against powder blue
radiant white beneath glazed cloud
whipped cream against froth
splash against pennant
white balloon against grey spray
butter yellow against toppled blue
thin blue against piled cloud
yellowed edge against blue billows

STATE HOUSE, AUGUST

torn shadow on blank white
blue glaze on heavy white
slate against falling down white
presence against white noise
dust bunny on meringue puffs
dust against smoke
hemp against cotton
tobacco against cotton
béchamel against pulled cotton
melting candle wax on brushed cotton
old button against flock
amber against lilac
enamel on formica
pearl against blue polished stone
tide-mark against bluestone
something poured on something backing away
resignation against cowardice
blessing before absolution
breath against gust
last smudge on erased page
incense smoke against steam
bleached linen against steam
stone against fleece
alabaster in cloud cauldron
charcoal against blue pennant
mouse fur against glass
marine blue against whale
shale in foam
froth against mist
[spume against drift]
dab against onslaught

STATE HOUSE, SEPTEMBER

retraction against foreboding
metal lid over blue-glazed plate
blue fingernails lilac clouds
scallop shell under floating cloud
scorched paper under slung smoke
sun-leap over madeleine
sunshine on a pale wall
petal on well water
readiness at first light
red-gold against glassy blue
shiny white against abalone
candle wax on rose
orange ice against faded denim
ice green against shining floes
dab against fervent blue
silver against grey
ermine against gauze
fur against mold
resignation against saturation
arthritis against glaucoma
cataracts on milky eyes
smooth palm on upper arm
palm against lint
plaque against swollen vein
exhaustion against anxiety

from *SOS Poetry* (2007)

"CRUMBLE TOUCH"

• Always arrive in town 2 years after property prices go up? You've got "CRUMBLE TOUCH."

• Always sign on the dotted line the day before interest rates come down? You may have "CRUMBLE TOUCH."

• Always on the wrong side of the cut-off date, rate, income, or city limit? Could you be a victim of "CRUMBLE TOUCH"?

• Too old to win the Yale Younger Poets even though your poetry is FUCKING BRILLIANT? The problem may be "CRUMBLE TOUCH."

• Have all your significant sexual relationships been with alcoholics and/or the mentally ill? Ever consider "CRUMBLE TOUCH"?

• Is life an unending struggle? Chances are you're riddled with "CRUMBLE TOUCH."

• Ever feel your luck has run out or was delivered to you in a leaky bag all those years ago? That's "CRUMBLE TOUCH."

HELP IS AT HAND

TAKE **"RIGIDITY"**: THE FIXATIVE FOR FIXING YOUR LIFE
PUT BACK-BONE IN YOUR FINGERTIPS
NO MORE "CRUMBLE TOUCH"
ROLL WITH THE PUNCHES LIKE A NINEPIN
LAUGH IN THE FACE OF THE FATES **HA-HA-HA-HA-HAH!**
BE DEVIL-MAY-CARE LET YOUR HAIR BLOW IN YOUR FACE AS
YOU ENJOY THE RIDE OF YOUR LIFE IN THE CONVERTIBLE
OF THE NEW YOU!
RIGIDITY! YOUR TICKET TO PEACHINESS
CARPE DIEM WITH A GOLDEN HANDSHAKE TODAY

THE EATEN BAGEL

THE EATEN BAGEL
Is swallowed by
The Designated
OWNER
Of THE EATEN BAGEL

(THE ONE to whom THE BAGEL
Is assigned
THE ONE who has THE RIGHT)

THE EATEN BAGEL is hidden
THE EATEN BAGEL is a lump in the throat
THE EATER *of* THE BAGEL is gleeful

THE EATEN BAGEL is secreted
All over THE BODY of THE
CONVERSATION *of* THE
BAGEL'S anticipation—

In THE CURVE between
CHIN & NECK

In **THE ARM-PIT**
Between THE BREASTS

THE EATEN BAGEL is
EATEN much more thoroughly
By its ANTICIPATOR

THE ONE
Who did not
EAT THE BAGEL

Than by the one who got to **EAT**
The **EATEN BAGEL**

SPRING

March
March
March
March
March
March
March
March
March
March
March
March
March
March
March
March
March
March
March
March
March
March
March
March
March
March
March
March
March
March
april

HUMIDITY

What is it?
It's the humidity.
No—what is it?
Humidity.
But what is it?
Humidity?
Oh what's humidity!
What's humidity!

WIND CHILL

What is it?
It's the wind chill.
No—what is it?
Wind chill.
But what is it?
Wind chill?
Oh what's wind chill!
What's wind chill!

WE ARE CHANGING OUR NAME

From: The Turners
To: The Grislingbums

From: Green Apple Press
To: Throg Sludge Books

From: DWGD Associates
To: DGWD Associates

From: Emoryville
To: Tebchaws

From: The Pipe & Sprocket Company
To: Shalalalala Unicorn

From: The Municipality of Bock
To: Txaizywjtxeeb

From: Miranda M. Brown
To: Mrs. Pit Nin

THINGS I'M GOOD AT

Smiling at children

[I intend to add to this list]

AT THE Y

fierce dark triangle
at junction of thighs
smooth body streaming
from cubicle—
oh glorious sight

MEET STEVE

This is Steve. Don't let the Anglo name fool you. Steve's name is really Stefan. And don't let that fool you either. Steve looks a lot like Franky G. in *Wonderland*. Uh-huh. Steve is a fireman and a realtor, both full-time.

Steve is a good-tempered man. He's not one to whine. Steve is the sort of guy who puts others' needs before his own. You know the type: he'll bring you chicken noodle soup in bed even when he's got the flu himself. He's just kind & generous & considerate. I know guys like Steve are a dime a dozen but for me there's just something kinda special about Steve.

Steve is also a part-time Dell technician. If you spill ginger ale on your laptop for example, Steve's your man. Steve runs a workshop from his backyard. There's very little he can't fix. Computers, cars, plumbing, electrical work: all fun & games to Steve. Steve is willing & able to help with light construction, insulation, window winterizing, any sort of painting & decoration, and of course—hauling out the garbage. He's a good cook and, from his time in the Navy, knows how to keep a kitchen— and a house—spick and span. Steve might be the only man you ever meet who'll gladly clean a toilet—and do a more thorough job than you.

Of course it's not all hard work & decency with Steve. He's a demon in bed. You know the sort of strong, powerful guy who's also very gentle. Very passionate, very sexual, very loving, very affectionate. He's one of those guys who can't stop cuddling. The only thing he likes more than a cuddle is a good chat. Or better still a simultaneous cuddle & chat. He's a hell of a listener, is Steve. Probably his strongest point however is his insatiable appetite for sex.

And he's a wonderful father. You know, one of those very loving, gentle men who spend time with their children, trying to put the little tykes first. I'm not saying it's easy but he's always there for them, even with the fireman and realtor jobs, the workshop in the garage, and bubble baths with me. He's just a truly great father. You know the type.

Well I guess you probably know a million guys like Steve so I won't go on and on about him. That's it from me.

DOOR

When you left
it was as if
one wall of the house
was taken down

I walked out
through that large door
into the carnival
world

SAVINGS

I know there's no money in the Checking Account.
I'm talking about the Savings Account.
No, not *that* Savings Account.
The Savings Account.
The Savings Account with the accumulated savings.
The one in the dark.
The one we don't touch.
The one behind the other one.
Remember?
The Savings Account behind the other Savings Account.
That one.
Yes.
How much is in there?

PEEL-A-WAY

The fear of black
peels away to lay bare
the fear of lead paint
peels away to lay bare
the fear of duplicity
peels away to lay bare
the fear of rats
peels away to lay bare
the fear of ruin
peels away to lay bare
the fear of cancer
peels away to lay bare
the fear of cruelty
peels away to lay bare
the fear of responsibility
peels away to lay bare
The fear of black

SINGLE MOTHER

I am the Easter Bunny
I am Santa Claus

DOWNTOWN CROSSING

A cup of coffee can be a mother.
A cigarette can be a mother.
A blanket can be a mother.
A wool cap can be a mother.
A coat can be a mother.
A booth can be a mother.
A warm grating can be a mother.
You can be your own mother.

TO CONQUER FEAR

Put a big prize on the other side of fear:

Heaven
On the other side of death

Home
On the other side of the snowstorm

An address
On the other side of this tangle of streets

THE DAY

Himalayan peaks
Smith Street
cucumber slice
44 West again
silver-grey light
my intersection my traffic light

PITCH

Okay so there's this poet—Gerard Manley Hopkins—who's a priest, a convert, his family are a little starchy about that, and he's marooned in Ireland for part of the movie. He does his best to be Welsh in Wales and Irish in Ireland but ends up dead of exhaustion and damp instead. And there's this other poet—Robert Bridges—and he's really mediocre and bombastic but what do you know he's incredibly successful and fêted and honored, poet laureate and everything, and get this: Gerard and Robert carry on a lifelong friendship. What do you think? Two poets, one (Bridges (hey maybe we could get Jeff Bridges to play him)) honored in his lifetime and completely forgotten now more or less. And the other (Hopkins (Bono? Ralph Fiennes? Marty Feldman? Martin Short?)) completely obscure in his lifetime but blazing like an acetylene torch right through the 20th century to the 21st. Can you see it? Ralph Fiennes as GMH slaving away grading papers in the depths of Newman House in the coldest wettest winter in Irish history. OK maybe uh John Lynch as Fr. Hopkins. Maybe uh that Heathcliffy guy Rufus Sewell. Hey maybe Helena Bonham Carter! That'd be something. Well definitely Bridges as Bridges. Sort of like *Thelma & Louise* slash *Chariots of Fire* slash *Fairies at the Bottom of the Garden* or whatever that movie was called—hey man this is **DYNAMITE!**

PITCH

Okay so there's this woman, let's say Catherine Zeta-Jones, and she's buying a house, so she finds this house and it's really beautiful, everything you could want so she goes to get a mortgage—no hang on—actually here's the thing: she's already pre-approved. So get this: *she's already pre-approved* but she doesn't have a realtor. She's found the house by herself. So okay now she has to find a realtor. That's the subplot. There's this realtor and that realtor—four realtors—and none of them works out until eventually she finds Sam (think Matthew Broderick so the chemistry's not there but there's a Johnny Depp type later on). Meanwhile the results of the inspection and appraisal come in and everything looks good. Okay so picture this: Catherine Zeta-Jones is saving furiously, can't even buy lunch anymore so she passes out at the check-out in *Au Bon Pain* just as she's counting pennies for coffee and she's revived by, you got it, the Johnny Depp type who is actually a banker standing in line. So he has the inside scoop on interest rates about to go down. They have lunch and she refinances at a better rate. Then the bomb hits: property taxes go up and Catherine's budget is out of whack. So Catherine and Matthew and Johnny all go down to City Hall where they meet with endless officials. Well that's really material for the sequel actually. The sequel is more of an action flick. This one is straight romance. What do you think?

PITCH

Okay. So it's the mid-17th century in Holland right. There's this ah 46-year-old fuzzy-headed arthritic maid-of-all-work and she goes to work in the home of a famous painter, sort of like Vermeer, actually it is Vermeer. And the 46-year-old fuzzy-headed arthritic maid-of-all-work and Vermeer develop this extraordinary friendship based on their mutual reverence for art. Yeah. Even though the fuzzy-headed 46-year-old arthritic maid-of-all-work is totally uneducated & poverty-stricken she just has this natural talent for composition & understanding the artist's soul. Vermeer recognizes it in her & reverences her for it. I mean Vermeer reverences her reverence for it right. But Vermeer the artist (thirtyish) is married to this 25-year-old woman who's already had like 5 children, 3 of whom have died and she's pregnant again. So Vermeer takes her great big pearl earrings & gives them to the maid-of-all-work so he can paint her portrait. For this patron. Who's a disgusting rapist character totally unlike the refined artist Vermeer. (Of course nobody remembers the patron's name. Van something or other.) So everybody thinks things are smoking up in the studio between the artist & the maid-of-all-work. But actually they're just mixing pigment & pointing out intricacies of light & shade. It's very beautiful. So in the end the painter gives the 46-year-old arthritic fuzzyheaded maid-of-all-work his wife's earrings. It's very realistic & shows how simple & profound reverence for art transcends class gender & all other barriers no problem what do you think?

ANOTHER SELF-PORTRAIT

pinwheels
pinwheels*pinwheels
PINWHEELS!!!PINWHEELS**!!!!****pinwheels!*******pinwheels***************
***************PINWHEELS!!!!!!!!!!!*pinwheels* ***pinwheels!
****pinwheels!!*********
PINWHEELS!!!!!!!PINWHEELS!!!!!!!!!*******PINWHEELS!!!!!!!!!!!!!!!!!!!!!!!!*******
*****PINWHEELS***********
pinwheels***PINWHEELS*************!!!!!!!!!!!!!!!!!!*PINWHEELS!!!!!**********
************************pinwheels
***************pinwheels***************************************
pinwheels!!!!PINWHEELS!!!!!!!****************PINWHEELS**********
pinwheels****pinwheels!****PINwheels!!!!!!pinWHEELS!!!!!!!!!!!!!!!!!!!!!!!!!!!!!!!!!!!!!P
INWHEELS!!!!!!!
!!!!!!!!!!!!
PINWHEELS!!!!!!!!!!!!!!!!!PINWHEELS*****************
PINWHEELS!PINWHEELS!!!!!!!!*************
*********PINWHEELS!***********

WHEN YOU KISS THE WORLD

in a poem

    you take its long throat

    & fuck

so deep

you come

    out

        laughing

        straight up

          into

            the bright face

            of

            God

AND FINALLY

I have never been sorry
to hear those words
at a poetry reading.

TRADITIONAL ~ IRISH ~ POEM

The next poem is a poem I got from a great fiddle-player James Kelly of Capel Street one night in Inis Oirr when he was out there playing with John Blake, a wonderful musician too. You might hear hints of a poet who has influenced us all Willie Yeats who had a castle there in Thoor Ballylee many's the grand night we had there with George and Anne and Michael a great family—that was before the summer school. And I'm indebted of course to Paddy Kavanagh from Iniskeen and Baggot Street, the sweetest melodeon player you ever did hear that used to play there up in McDaid's and Nesbitt's I was there hanging on every note. And all the great sessions around Dublin and Dundalk that are recorded on the old 78s I remember the excitement when a new batch of them would be brought home and fair play to all the men and women who collected them. It's through them I heard the music of Allen Ginsberg of Newark New Jersey and Alan Dugan from Brooklyn New York and Allen Grossman in Baltimore there and Alan Sondheim of Manhattan Island and all the Allens, a magnificent family, second only to the Alices. And Charles Reznikoff a great walker also of New York, and Harry Crane from Chagrin Falls and Sukey Howe—her mother was a *Manning*—and Fanny her sister, felicitous poets both, and May Swenson that we all loved and Muriel too, and Langston Hughes up there in Harlem, I tried to get him to come to Áras Éanna many's the time but no dice and Gus Young in London and Trevor Joyce who published Gus and Trevor's Uncle Jimmy a truly great poet though not necessarily when he said so and Marcel Duchamp and Pierre Reverdy and Artie Rimbaud and Paul Muldoon his *Incantata* was only massive and Paul Celan with his *Todesfuge* and Paulie Durcan from Leinster Square a very prolific poet and all the Pauls, another great family. And Tom Raworth God bless him and Hugo Ball and Randolph Healy from outside Bray and Mícheál O hAirtnéid from Newcastlewest no longer with us unfortunately but a wonderful poet and player we remember fondly and Ger Hopkins that used work up there in Newman House on his sprung rhythm and Eavan out in Dundrum many's the cup of coffee I had at her kitchen counter and Crystal Williams I played with her in the Big Red Barn one time at Cornell it was powerful and Rachel Loden in San Francisco and Gabriel Gudding with whom I wrote *The Clio Reel* some of you may know it we're still dancing to that one. So for all the men and women of poetry and John Donne here goes:

from *An Educated Heart* (2005)

BAGHDAD

They come, we stop them and we pound them and they go and when we stop they return.
—Iraqi Minister of Information, Mohammed Saeed al-Sahaf, April 5, 2003

if I leave Baghdad early towards Baghdad will never reach Baghdad will never come to Baghdad are nowhere near Baghdad not near Baghdad **near Baghdad** armoured push towards Baghdad approached Baghdad push into Baghdad advance on Baghdad forces drove into Baghdad in the raid into Baghdad probing mission in Baghdad not even 100 miles from Baghdad 10 miles from central Baghdad just seven miles from Baghdad on the outskirts of Baghdad to make it into Baghdad home to Baghdad fly on into Baghdad home free to Baghdad little more than one hour from Baghdad an hour and a half short of Baghdad encirclement of Baghdad siege of Baghdad to choke Baghdad cut Baghdad in half so to speak pulled back to Baghdad back to Baghdad highway to Baghdad main road going into Baghdad main road going into Baghdad to Baghdad on Baghdad to Baghdad over Baghdad fleeing Baghdad sky over parts of Baghdad on what parts of Baghdad vast areas of Baghdad south-east of Baghdad into southern Baghdad Baghdad's southern Baghdad from the east south-western areas of Baghdad beyond north-west of Baghdad from southern Baghdad They're in Baghdad actually in the city of Baghdad inside Baghdad in central Baghdad in the heart of Baghdad in the heart of Baghdad penetrate the heart of Baghdad into the centre of Baghdad to smash rocked the centre of Baghdad stacked up over Baghdad enveloping Baghdad penetrating Baghdad isolated Baghdad swept low over Baghdad thrust into Baghdad night-time bombing of Baghdad the people of Baghdad had the poor of Baghdad the people of Baghdad deserted streets of western Baghdad in the streets of Baghdad on a house in Baghdad's **street dogs of Baghdad** convoy out of Baghdad Battle of Baghdad All across Baghdad vast areas of Baghdad vast areas of Baghdad vast, flat city of Baghdad Baghdad's hospitals liberated Baghdad *Hi you guys. I'm in Baghdad* outside Baghdad inside Baghdad Baghdad burning 18 blue and black arrows around Baghdad fell on Baghdad head out of Baghdad Leaving Baghdad history of Baghdad As we left Baghdad

TRAPPED

house is trashed. near the ruined market. thick crust of sand.
render non-existent whole buildings by remote control. destroying
all six houses. breaking nearly every window on the street. demolishing
burning ramshackle auto repair shop. gutting small diner. destroying.
burn to death inside their car. school damaged bombs detonated above
a residential home.   school. tearing apart top floor. shrapnel. and breaking
most of school's windows. strewn with wreckage. bloodstains on a
            sidewalk. blood-soaked children's slippers. water
            seeping   ruptured pipes. corrugated iron said
                                            dangling
        from roofs of damaged shops. " " umbilical wires and
            broken concrete. trapped under   rubble.
        screamed demolished office and several nearby
                                    houses. said
        turned block " " into rubble rubble from the smashed
and smoldering hit rattling windows of a gaping gash slammed
into homes and shops buildings into charnel houses. twisted metal.
rubble everywhere. rest is ashes.

RUBBLE

dug through **rubble** frantically **rubble** strewn over marble split open like dolls' houses
cut down inside living room brick hut single-storey corrugated iron and cement
two-room brick right through windows walls shaking building shake
bombed
house.   hundreds of small holes in the walls of the upstairs
roof patio.
broken glass at the
entrance, we entered _____
in Baghdad.   rooms are   disarray. Several walls cracked,
windows all shattered and a thick layer of dust/grime
exposed furniture, books, carpets and floors.
windows shattered and the
doors were blown out.
rubble
hospital destroyed bombs missing in **rubble** were
buried this morning crumpled
crushed windows of sixteen all broken crouching in **rubble**
gaping windows and wrecked houses windows blew
in
blows out all the glass from the windows damage
to windows **rubble**
from walls large blood stained mattress on floor
crushed in **rubble** of farmhouse
pulverized by missiles with
built of soft brown stone, and the explosion
house's outer walls like butter
small crater and pockmarks of shrapnel damage scattered across house walls
grey-powdered **rubble**

METAPHOR, SIMILES

like grapes from the sky

like small grapefruit

metal butterflies

like small stones

like cough sweets in a metal sheath

like a treehouse

like dolls' houses

like butter

like a bell with a very hollow ring

like a doll in a funeral shroud

like heavy wooden furniture being moved in an empty room

HEADLINES

TINY ORGASM POPS OVER BAGHDAD
PERSONS RISK GENTLENESS
WOMAN BRINGS MAN TO BRINK AS MISSILES LAUNCH
NO SEX SAYS PRESIDENT SINCE 1993
TROOPS SEEK PRIVACY TO HANDLE COCKS
STRANDED BODY PARTS WEEP
BRIT SEMEN SPARKS DESERT FLOWER
PILOT NAVIGATES BY VAGINAL ACHE
FINGER SLIPS INTO INTIMATE ZONE
CITY RUMMAGED FOR GUERILLA KISS

ALMOST

Suicide Bomber Almost Kills 50 at Police Station in Iraq (REUTERS)
Guerrilla Raid in Restive Iraq Town Leaves 22 Almost Dead (REUTERS)
Moscow Pool Roof Collapse Almost Kills 26, Search Goes On (REUTERS)
China Shopping Mall Fire Almost Kills at Least 53 (REUTERS)
U.S. Soldier Almost Dies, Five Held in Iraq Council Killing (REUTERS)
Four U.S. Troops Wounded, Iraqi Almost Killed in Ambush (REUTERS)
Palestinian Suicide Bomber Almost Kills 8 in Jerusalem (REUTERS)
Rumsfeld Assesses Iraq Security; Bomb Almost Kills 13 (REUTERS)
Nearly 600 Almost Killed in Powerful Morocco Quake (REUTERS)
Iraq Leaders Call for Calm After Attacks Almost Kill 165 (REUTERS)
More Than 20 Almost Killed in Attacks on Pakistan Shi'ites (REUTERS)
Six Palestinians Almost Die in Failed Attack on Israelis (REUTERS)
Baltimore Water-Taxi Capsizes, 2 Almost Dead, 3 Missing (REUTERS)
Six Almost Killed in Anti-Aristide March in Haiti (REUTERS)

CHOOSE YOUR HUSBAND

War Activist: *You should be shot in the head*
Peace Activist: *No. You should be shot in the head*

CROP

I THOUGHTXXXXXXXXXXXXXXXX
XXXXXXBECAUSE YOU SAW ME
XXXXXXXXXSLICED &XXXXXXXXX
XXXXXXXXXXTORN OPENXXXXXX
XXXXXXXXXXX&XXXXXXXXXXXX
XXXXXTHE SHINING CHILDXXXXX
XXXXXXXXXXDRAGGED FROM ME
XXXXXXYOU WOULD HAVEXXXXX
XXXSTAYED WITH USXXXXXXXXX
XXXXXXXXXXFOR LIFEXXXXXXXX
XXXXXXXXXXXXXXXXXXXXXXXX
XXXXXXXXXBUT NOT SOXXXXXXX

TEDIUM

I park the green car in the rain and go in the red door to collect my child:
My child whose face is a white petal detaching and fluttering toward me.
I park the green car under the clouds and go in the red door for my child:
My child whose dark hair falls over her head as she bends to her drawing.
I park the green car in the tight sun and go in the red door to collect my child:
My child deep in a cluster of children sticking colored paper to paper:
My child who shouts out: *Can I finish this first?* I am thinking about divorce.
I park the green car in the sun and go in the red door to collect my child:
My child who hurtles toward me/I swing her around/then Yang-Yang hurtles towards me/
I swing Yang-Yang round/Her father is coming in nine days to take her.
I park the green car in the rain and go in the red door for my child:
My child who stands by the wall in the gymnasium with other wallflowers hanging her head.
I park the green car in the rain and go in the red door for my child:
My child pounding the floor of the gymnasium with her strong little calves.
I park the green car in the sun and go in the red door for my child:
My child who is not in the cafeteria/and not in the gymnasium/and not in the first playground
But there—in the kindergarten playground on the slide—upside down is my child.
I park the green car in the sky and go in the red door for my child:
My child whose face is a white petal detaching and fluttering towards me.

THE WAY OF THE WORLD

The soldier met the woman halfway.
"You killed my daughter," she said.
"Yeah, I'm sorry about that," the soldier replied.
"But do you remember when I asked you for water
you refused me—
you wouldn't treat a dog like that.
So I'm sorry about your daughter—
I hope you're sorry about the water too."
"It's not the same thing," said the woman.
"Not to you maybe," said the soldier.
"But who can account for how another person feels?"
 "You raped and killed my daughter," said the woman.
"I didn't rape her. We had consensual sex."
"She was six."
"Look, there are mistakes on both sides.
We both have to live with that.
Your daughter is gone, get over it.
What I could use from you right now is water."

A LOVING AUDIENCE IS NECESSARY

and then oh my god and then suddenly jeepers I nearly
what do you think but what should I what should we
do you think we you won't believe I was oh my god
you know how well it was like that remember that
was anyway it was like when remember when
do you think we what if we don't
do you will you really it was scary oh my god
you know how well you know how so
look at you there I was you can imagine well
guess what hey baby hey my sweetheart what
about you though will you be do you think we
will we be it's a with you us us
we could we may do you think we let's let's what
do you think should we or we might oh my god
you know how well it was like
that it was crazy you know how

AN EDUCATED HEART

El cora-zon-ed-u-cado
Huay   de shing
  ↑ schuay ↓ ↑
     ↓
Hway shoo-eh deh sheeng
Gyo yook eui mah eum
Kyeogh yuke oo-eh mah-um
Oon Cŏ–rah-sŏn Ehh–doo–că–dŏ
Croí foghlamtha
Croí eolasach
Croí oilte
Croí feasach
Ein gebildetes hertz
Hertzenbildung
Un coeur savant
Un ker savan
Oon cohdahsohn e-thoo-kah-thoh
Oon cor-ath-sone eh-doo-ca-dho
Meu coração educādo
Mih cora-sew ee-duc-ad-oo
Hui Xin
Huay shing
Kyōyōnoaru kokoro

from *Nelson & the Huruburu Bird* (2003)

A VOW OF POETRY

Mairéad went into town with her brothers and sisters one day. There was a funfair in O'Connell Street and they all had money in their pockets. Seán went on the orange and red helter-skelter. Eamonn played roll-a-penny. Sheila had her fortune told by a little chest-high effigy wearing a scarf. The girls linked arms and flounced up and down the street. Then they all had candy floss. No one noticed that Mairéad was missing, but after a while she turned up beside them again. She had been to the little pitched canvas tent in the centre of the street and taken a vow of poverty. Years later, at one of their regular uproarious gatherings, the brothers and sisters got to talking about this day. Mairéad mentioned her vow of poverty. "A little pitched tent? I never noticed that," they all said. Until Deirdre remembered: "Oh no, Mairéad, I know what you're talking about. That wasn't *poverty*, that was *poetry!*" "Oh," said Mairéad, "I assumed the *v* was hidden in a fold in the canvas. What a mistake! I feel such a fool to have remained poor all these years! And all the time it was *poetry!*"

THE PILLAR

I am now only a captain but I will, if I live, be at the top of the tree.
—Horatio Nelson to Sir William Hamilton

Clouds scud, what else, in the grey sky, and yes,
gulls hang all the way out, to the bay, I guess,
the river neck, and the sky lets loose
bannerfuls of rain, hail, snow, tumbleweeds
of darkness, cold; that old familiar drizzle
emptying the dawn, down all the days,
the yellow city nights; and his head sleek
like a lizard, like a cobra, like a basilisk
inserted in our heavens, in the bells'
clamor, clangor, Nelson, lord of us all.

We were low, no supposing, low-down in our boots,
battering past the pillar's base, clattering into this ravine
or that, clip-clopping up the gulch of North Earl
Street, step after step lapping at the shop fronts
like a tide coming in, inexorable, not to be baulked.
Dwarfed by the buildings of what was Sackville,
then O'Connell, stranded now, the hug of the crowd
slackened, light-headed, wondering *where's me bus* and
which side of the road am I on, stunned to find life
in the shape of big lit buses, tattered queues, going on;
ready to plunge at the drop of a hat or a hand into a blue
funk or stock taken, bearings found, Henry Street,
the gorge chock-a-block, rain melting down its windows,
and the women's rough mouths like O's roaring *Toblerone* or
Get the last of this or that *Cheeky Charlies* don't you know
the whole street rocking underneath the red and yellow shock
of neon on its bedrock of black and the double bass of feet thudding
all the way down to Mary Street, the smell of wet fur.
So this was *dubh le daoine* and we were shoulder to shoulder
ag baint dhá thaobh den bóthar, drink or no drink, for sure,
we were *íseal*, right enough, as *íseal as íseal* could be
beneath our *uasal*, casting his long shadow on us, and we
in our stew, in our soup, in our mate and potatoes mess.

Woolworths was a box of light. On the bright side
looking out you could see the streaked street,
plate glass doors like a fresco, Jackson
Pollock maybe on a dark day or better still
the tubes of paint themselves, melting.
On the inside Hopper but all pastels.
Or the Gobi Desert. There was no shade.
Fluorescence had the say-so; boy how it swam
across the insulated ceilings from the steaming
entrance to the back of the store where you got
your picture taken with no front teeth. How it lit
with one blast the whole shebang; it
was horizontal and vertical, spilled
like a sheet down and in and out and on
the downy heads of the assistants
with their warm crests of hair. Or the hoity
toity girls at make-up, maxfactored
or revloned, their perfect fingers tapping,
one mascaraed eye on the clock, or on the mirror
where it tilted on the countertop,
reflecting glass and chrome glass and chrome
all the way back to where I stood
in my mittens in my knitted bobble-cap
the two pounds ten for presents
in the *póca* of *mo chóta* my toggle coat.
Here were bath cubes, dense in their silver jackets,
talcum powder for the nun or a sewing kit
for mama, bubble bath and soap
shaped like swans or seashells, strings of pearls,
garden gnomes and cupids, watchstraps for the dada,
all the bounty of the age of plastic but regulated, oh yeah.
At the sweet counter girls drift
peach cheeks turned clean nails deep
in rayon coveralls. Here were heaps.
Piled in lots of spangles dolly mixtures lemon drops
and the little pewter shovels riding
up the hills of toffee, hunks of broken chocolate.

Here were paper bags and spillages,
the lone sweet escaped or caught in the wrong mix
pressed against the perspex or fallen in the crevices,
and down on the floor, more, maybe two or four,
hanging, where the floor and counter meet,
in their shiny wrappers, red and gold, and your baby fingers curl
and your tongue shifts and your eyes
bigger than your belly, popping from the back of your head
two eyes and one in the middle of your forehead
like Balor, like Medusa, who could turn a man to stone.

He was there when we drove like snakes into all that mess
that gorgeousness. He was there on his pockmarked stone
when we jumped off the bus's tail-end.
He was there when the wind and the hail and the snow
God knows came rattling from the sky and the apple-pie girls
brown thighs pumping and the pipe bands marched by
and the white smiles of JFK and Jackie flashed
at ten thousand shivering stars and stripes when
the auld triangle went a-jingle-jangle,
he was there, he was there, he was there.
When we were ten or eleven and hobbled with Miss D
up the street past the penny arcades and the fortune-teller
nodding and the woman screeching *Hail
Queen of Heaven* white hair swept up
in an ice-cream cone. Past Fortés and Worth's
past the Happy Ring House and Clery's
to the Monument Cafe where we ate stale buns
drank tea milked and sugared with all the milk and sugar
on the white Formica table so we'd get our money's worth.
And the dreadful smell of city centre churches.
Those were long dry summers coasting mildly
down to queues outside *An Gúm* or Gills
and the sniff of new school *nua-Ghaeilge* new hist'ry books.

He was there all that time and before that time.
He was there through Cinerama and Panorama and Senssurround

He was there in all the pantomimes
He was there for *Strumpet City*
He was there on the Abbey stage before it burnt down
He was there for the *Plough* and there for the *Stars*
He was there in the wings when the women ran with prams
when the gunboat *Helga* when *Ulysses*
when the street broke and the poets stumbled
with a white flag and James Connolly from the GPO.

He was there for the Eucharistic Congress
when McCormack sang *Panis Angelicus*
for the Pope's man at the mass for the masses
in O'Connell Street and my mother's mother
six months a widow there too our new freedom
sure enough. He was there on the Feast every year
when the folks from the country came up
with their parcels of eggs for the city cousins
and their cash he was there when they fumbled
there when they groped there for all the talk
of snails and slime and *how far have we gone
and how far to go one hundred thirty four feet
can you bate that look you can see the people through the cracks.*
He was there at the top when they stuck
their puckered foreheads out, craned their necks,
laid their giant hands on railings, counted churches,
thought of Eiffel maybe or the Statue of Liberty
how the Phoenix Park was the largest park in Europe,
O'Connell Street the broadest street
Jack Doyle the champion of the world
and wasn't DeValera the right quare name.

For he never went with Phipps to the Arctic Ocean
He never chased the bear nor was the light-haired boy
nor sailed to the East Indies nor saw two hundred floggings
nor blew a cold north wind among the isles of the West Indies
He never routed privateers from Montego to Honduras
nor terrorized Americans as captain of the *Boreas*

saw Yellow Jack take all but ten of *Hichinbrooke's* two hundred
nor loved his men was loved by them nor raced his little middleshipmen
nor fought for Hood nor crossed Lord Keith
nor lost an eye at Calvi an arm at Tenerife
in the dog-days in the lion sun nor his heart to Lady Hamilton
nor ran Napoleon to ground at Alexandria
nor saw the boy stand on the burning deck
nor watched the *Orient* go up nor heard the silence after
nor lynched Caracciolo nor swaggered round as Bronte
nor saw the *lazzaroni* loose their birds in tribute to his victory
nor ditched his wife nor had a child
nor said that *fifty naked virgins would not tempt* him
nor *money is trash*
nor *I shall perhaps be hanged. Let them!*
nor squashed the Danish fleet at Copenhagen
nor never saw the signal to stop firing
nor held the glass to his blind eye saying
Foley I really cannot see it
Keep mine for closer battle flying! Nail mine to the mast!
Nor prayed for laurel or cypress
nor chased Villeneuve and Gravina to and from the Caribbean
nor met them at Trafalgar and got his pell-mell battle
nor walked and turned on the quarter-deck
walked and turned in the smoke
walked and turned with his gold stars glinting
till the rifleman on the mizentop
broke his back with a ball
nor hid his face and stars nor said
I'm a dead man, Hardy. Kiss me.

For he never lived and died
but stood landlocked on his perch on his plinth on his pillar
in the rain in the sun in the great massy light
till the day he went up up up
spewing rock spewing stone
spitting mugs and jugs and stars and bars
schooners cutters frigates

geegaws ribands chunks of his own leaden coffin
and the tatters of the flag the sailors tore
relics of Saint Nelson and the roar of grief
for Baron Nile and Crocodile Viscount Pyramid
Duke of Thunder and Burnham Thorpe
Burnham Westgate Burnham Market Burnham Overy
Burnham Ulph Burnham Norton Burnham Sutton
Burnham Deepdene Burnham St Andrew Burnham Harbour
all the Burnhams and the ships of the line
Carcass Racehorse Seahorse Albemarle Agamemnon Elephant Vanguard Victory
holds of gold of plate the gates of Valetta
Cathedral and the twelve apostles in molten silver rained down
with tanners coppers oyster shells
and a few plum stones
and the larks were singing straight out of the shocked trees
Our Nel Our Nel Our Nel

The Pillar had shot its wad
and we stood in its spume
knee-deep in rubble
not knowing to take credit or what.
The stump was still frothing
and there for the taking
spilled all around
was granite shiny and sandy:
Easy to bend down and slide
deep in a pocket a hand or an eye.

I knew all the hiding places of our house.
Or most. Or some. The warm bedclothes
where sunshine and myself could lie.
The children's cries outside—*I* was a child—
The covers of a book! The empty rooms
when all the family was out. Dusk, darkness
lustrous as a wing enveloping the house.
My father's pockets mother's purse
the cubbyhole under the stairs the beds the coats

the hollow base of bookshelves where
we laid flat coppers for someone sometime to find—
the oblong slots beneath the floorboards
deep enough to stash a man. The old kitchen
inside the new—I see its lines—
and feel its angles still, not gone
but undisclosed like bones—the recess in
the attic wall where in a brown binoculars case
I hid terrazzo from the old hall floor
a brass capsule that held St. Christopher
and Nelson's rock: this scrap, this jolt,
forget-me-not, down-drop, I posted
through the wall and nudged and lost the lot.

And of this town. The pubs inside the pubs
made new to look like old or old made look like new
the pints and pints and pints each daisy-fresh
and sloppy on the bar. The shops inside the shops
or stores and malls and billboards where
I waited on the corner for her daddy son or holy ghost,
jabbed in the ribs by what or who was not, no longer, there.
He ran, that alley, and that window there, blue light was where
you might be born or get it in the back.
Ní bheidh, they say, our *leithéid*, yet it's thronged,
throat-cluttered with the looks, the blinks, the pulled-back
glance, ahems, the fat cigars or pipes or nervous cigs
of all the winners, losers on these streets, the sorry plaque
on Anna Livia, foot-drift on rude tarmac or pavement ruffle,
cherished space, gulls hang and Nelson soars
and we rise up and kneel, rise up and kneel again.

ORDNUNGS

On the quays   the window of the house   where I lived is open
  and the curtain   if there is a curtain   blows
birds   yes there are birds   fly in   out
  and you walk past   and I walk past   this window   other windows

Who, if I cried—said Rilke   and Berryman said he was a jerk.
  And Dugan said that Berryman was a jerk   for saying   Rilke was a jerk.
My guess is that they were all jerks   with their jerky and strategic cries—
  save Dugan   who is   after all   alive.

I could take you by the hand and lift you vertically   from street to sill
  show you the undulating floor   half-open inner door   the hint of   staircase
leading to a room   knee-deep in paper   where a girl waits
  cheek-to-pane   for the stranger below   to come up.

Who   do the redundant cables   on the flagpoles   along the Liffey clank for now?
  Let's not talk of derelict space   the tacky paint in layers
but the active ears of listeners   snug   in custom-built apartments
  all the way down to the Four Courts   their paper-thin walls.

I stand   elbows on the river-wall   on the south side   looking north—
  the lemon strings of curtain smash against   blue brick.
My poem has gathered herself   and removed to some place else:
  I'm the poorest person in this room, empty-throated, truculent.

CYCLING TO MARINO

Leaves and leaves and leaves—
huge chestnut fans, bright sycamore, and oak
plastered against pavement, kerb, cushioning slick road
beneath my tires, stifling the slight squirt of rain
which should mark my passing.

My sisters I've cast off, shed them at the turn
up Glandore Road, and I continue free-
wheeling on the stretch of Griffith Avenue that's mine
until I hit the school. I'm seven and exultant in the drowse
of leaves, thick colors, dormancy, fine rain.

In the classroom, the heat from hot water pipes
dries sodden clothes on skin. We know someone's
not clean, and someone's poor, and always late,
someone's too fat or tall or pale
and someone's palms get reddened much too often
but what does poor mean? Where are those places
other people live? Places to the north or east
with names like Artane, Donnycarney, Whitehall—
houses much like our own but not, strange
mothers making stew in sculleries while we
swim through the classroom,
absorbing drench and drift—

Metallic taste of ink on lips so much more urgent even
than the waxy paper bread and jam
comes wrapped in. Or glimpse of stacks
of brand-new copies, unpared pencils bound
with bands, lodged deep within the unlocked cupboard.
Delirium of new books, bold colors barely dry,
the smell of pages fresh from printing works
while we sit chewing wood or graphite, wool,
the whorls on fingertip soak up
the business of the day, eyes clinging to the nun's
soft winter habit, the way the pleat turns
at her breast, the independent curve of strand, of thread,

the heavy cross along the length of robe
that's petrol blue. We're learning how to sew, to knit,
each stitch has singularity, then holds its shape
in partnership with the next, and next—

My mother walks along the avenue to meet me.
She carries apples. And I dismount,
escorting her through bowers that I know best,
stern arch of branch, cascade of leaf,
the stench of fermentation, rain.
We planted bulbs today—I could try this—
how I wished to drive my sharp white teeth
against brown jackets into compact flesh!
Today I broke my flask. I hear its subdued rattle
in my bag and I am scared, seeing ahead
her glass-roofed kitchen, home,
keeping to myself my own disasters or
the sight of silver shards abandoned
in a pool of milky tea, the way tea leaks
into the awkward gloss of concrete,
the way steam rises in snarls,
mysterious, remote like heat, then disappears.

ELEGY WITHOUT TOOTH OR HEART

Your mother shaved your head
when you had lice and sent
you back to school, a small
bald thing with worried eyes—
even your friends were ashamed.
Both of your mothers were brutes.
That's the God's honest truth—
one pushed you out, one took you in;
they did what had to be done.
There were men in there somewhere, it's true.
There were at least two,
not counting the one who smashed you up,
and that was an accident too.
I remember you best in your coffin.
Your sins were forgiven—
that much was clear
from the care the nuns took
in dolling you up.
You looked like a cross
between Old Mother Hubbard,
Christ's Bride,
and the Massacre of the Innocents,
all decked out in lace and blue fingernails,
with hand-sewn decorations in your head,
you were dead, Rosemarie.
There was a crowd of us there.
I knelt on the suave terrazzo floor
that was streaked with December slush.
I swayed on my great potato knees
and prayed to the Paraclete
for tongues of flame and miracles.
Of course nothing happened.
I smelt every ointment anyone used
and who drank and what old woman sucked drops.
My father, behind me, broke out his life's stock of tears.

Everyone's clothes were wet,
perhaps even yours,
where they hadn't quite closed you up.
The stink rose and it didn't include
the last of your little girl smells.
You still embarrassed us all.
Plucked, patched, dead as a dodo,
even the glamour of being an orphan
had gone to the bad
because the ending was grim.
I idolized and survived you.
And *hey you* I have a daughter.
I named her for you, and water.

POSTNATAL WARD

It sure was intimate.
I meet women I knew then
and we don't even say hello.
I knew when their bowels moved,
when their breasts leaked,
what and how much they liked to eat,
what sorts of husbands they had
and how often,
the stuff they were made of,
how much money they had in the bank,
but seldom their names.
I knew their babies—
they were gazed at, compared.
I swear that I thought
each one as amazing as mine.
I inspected the ranks—
the monkey-faced one incubated,
the twins, the red-headed guy with the scabs,
the feminine boys and my masculine girl,
my spanking-new fat-legged girl!
My next-door-bed-neighbor was deaf.
Her husband and children would visit:
stream in and spread out on her bed
a fiesta of rough diamond talk.
I knew the snobs,
the ones who cut off,
the women who'd been there before
and the ones who fell down adoringly before Christ
in thanks for their child,
the women lying in pain
the ones who were clipped
the big women who loved
who were wheeled in at night,
stunned and rekindled each time
they remembered their child.
There was no shortage of pain,
of loss, of silence, of death.

We were the elected,
the chosen few.
We were the *crème de la crème.*
My breasts spouted milk.
My whole body swaggered—
casual about its great coup.
It was so bloody glamorous!
My baby slept like a nun
in no rush to let the world in.
I outstared the night,
watched Dublin turn yellow and navy and pink,
and surging through me were giant peals of joy, joy, joy—
and I couldn't wait to get out.

EARLY MORNING, DUBLIN

The sweet substantial smell of fermentation rolls
across the city from the brewery. I'm wheeling my bicycle
up Christchurch, steering toward the geriatric hospital
where I'm the youngest orderly, the thinnest, and the loneliest.
Or I'm hearing my own footsteps all the way along Capel Street,
ghostly and cavernous as darkness lifts and morning is left shivering,
unsure. Then taking the turn down Mary's Abbey to the markets,
just to see the banks of flowers, row on row, before
suburban grocers pack them in their cars and head
for Harold's Cross, Dundrum, Drumcondra.
Stopping for tea and toast at the one café that's open,
or settling in for a pint at an early house,
thick with the fug of a pub that never closes, except
on Christmas and Good Friday *(the two days of all the year
when we could use a pint)*, stripping the cellophane
from a twenty pack of cigarettes, harboring myself.

Or I'm coming home from a night shift, not through
north city squares where seagulls walk along the paths
of locked parks, not to my childhood home, my mother's house,
but to the homes I've found, high on Henrietta Street
where white birds scatter against the blank face of the King's Inns.
Or home along the quays, cutting through Liffey Street,
past shuttered shops, past loaded skips, and papers blowing.
I'm carrying a pound of rashers, butter, from another hospital
where I'm obliged to steal *(to cover for the one
I cover for)*. And I'm a vegetarian. And we don't have a fridge.
Or I am empty-handed coming home, dilute as the traffic lights
which blink on empty streets. I'm leaving *The Mad Carver*,
or some other all-night dive, where I have drunk
and smoked and waited for Dolores, Lynn,
all the prostitutes whose names I have forgotten,
remembering only the murdered and disgraced.

GROOMING

for Marina

I brush with your father's soft silver brush,
which you love, for it smoothens the surface,
asks no questions, like his hands, hurriedly
settling, before lighting a cigarette.

Then with my brush, which you hate, difficult
fingers rake, immune to your cries, insistent
on manifest destiny, *idée fixe*
of encroachment, *I will know, I will know.*

I take up the fine-tooth comb, snout nosing
blankly along white runnels of scalp, north
to south, snuffling for inroads, thrust back
again and again by covert refusal of hair.

I change tack, airlift from the interior,
send foot patrols out, skirmishing on the perimeter,
stalking unfurrowed brow, skirting the pools
your forehead exudes — your hairline presses
out beads like the crowns of the princesses
you draw — as silence falls down

and I come to the delicate country
at the back of your neck, my Burren flower,
damp tropics at the down-covered nape,
my only one, exposing the mauvish inlet,
naive skin, candid hollow (which took
such ages to cover) to risk of the sun.

I lift molten strands, copper straps, oxblood
ribbons, I sift and I pin, caught in the task
of placement, displacement, separation
a dream that evades until,
abandoning instruments, I plunge in,
I handle your warm weight of hair,
rummage through it, meditative as a cat

remembering the ache of this head—or
was it this head—under my ribs before
birth, then the rudeness of passage
and after, when it still needed propping,
already turned from me, neck red and stunned
with milk, this head which I almost own!

remembering long afternoons in the schoolroom,
slow storage of heat from high windows
hair heavy as a hat on my listening head

lulled now, resistance to blunt fingertip
fades to nudge slips to shift at my touch

I unfold skein after skein, layer loosing
layer, lustrous fiber, tessellation
sans syntax, blonde heliograph, amber
chatter, crisscross of russet on gold,
burnished chaos, semiotics of shafts'
gleam and glint, now, at its most maddening,
the hair opens up to me,
yields from its mass the particular
rhythm of the singular hair
like a poem from debris of drafts
child from the pit of birth
it seems that at last I can know
one living hair of your head, for nothing
to the diligent expert is impossible,
my consort my familiar my mate.

At night you lie finished beside me,
heaped on our bed, sculpted
in light from uncurtained windows,
inviolate as marble,
anointed at forehead and throat
with the rank oil of the mother,
sleep clothing each exit and entrance
that morning gives access to —

the imperious voice has turned in,
imperious finger that points
to this button, that nail,
collaborative silence that submits
to my stroking, fastidious
naming of parts —

And still your fingers furl towards me,
still the incessant winkling of time,
involuntary donorship of parts.
I trade my red meat for all your soft substances,
your harvests of hair and skin.
You repay your debts in scales and secretions
and a threat *that you will always sleep with me,*
your blood pulsing onward as I relapse

afraid to look at your milk-teeth
to mark the first signs of decay

And still your fingers furl towards me,
while your head, hair tied tightly back,
bent in dream, explodes on a vision
of *Adam and Niamh,* as you hear it,
gallantly naked and riding the waves,
Niamh's golden hair whipping round them,
astride her white mare and galloping
from Paradise to the Land of Youth.

The bright diadem breaks out!
You sort through the myths I have funneled you
for fear you might think I am God.

REFLEX

It is not, after all, the water,
slate of the bay, nor the promontory,
curve of the regulated city,
salt rush, that I miss,
nor heading out somewhere with you.

It is more some things which never
got a name, that tin with thread,
the yoke for holes,
a cheap copybook,
I am at a loss for now.

Until, in a room, the full
lips of a stranger
catch in sumptuous dip—
the shutter flies open on you.
Then the tears let down.

A SALUTE TO THE CAPE VERDEAN COMMUNITY IN BOSTON: COMMENTS IN A VISITORS' BOOK

for Beverley Conley

"Be very proud.
It is ten grains of dust
that God spread over the ocean.
It is ours but we didn't take it by fighting.
It's Cape Verde, beloved country."

"My people are from Brava, I've never been,
my dad came here when he was twenty-one,
born in Fogo, raised in Brava.

My mom's folks came here
a year before I was born.

I cherish all they've given me."

"Your pictures bring me back
to a place I've never been—

Brava, the most quietest place on earth."

"You make us prouder.
My people! My land!
Today I feel as though Boston finally accepts me."

"Love is coming very soon."

DIRECTIONS FOR *THE DEAD*

SNOW FALLING ON THE OUTSKIRTS OF THE CITY.
                    DISSOLVE TO:
SNOW FALLING ON A VAST LANDSCAPE.
                    DISSOLVE TO:
SNOW FALLING ON BARE HILLS.
                    DISSOLVE TO:
SNOW FALLING ON A BOG.
                    DISSOLVE TO:
SNOW FALLING INTO THE TURBID WATERS OF A LARGE RIVER.
                    DISSOLVE TO:
A DISTANT HILL WITH A LONELY CHURCHYARD AT THE TOP.

CLOSER SHOT OF CHURCHYARD.

SNOW LYING THICKLY DRIFTED ON CROOKED CROSSES AND HEADSTONES.
SNOWS LYING ON THE SPEARS OF THE LITTLE GATE.
SNOW FALLING ON A DESERTED BIRD'S NEST.
SNOW FALLING ON ONE SPECIFIC GRAVE.
SNOW FALLING ON BARREN THORNS.
TILT UP TO INFINITE SNOW FALLING.

                    FADE OUT:

                THE END

FOR THE EAR OF THE AUDITOR

So it is you after all!

What I had in mind was a hall
a mountain of dark
a tarn
and somewhere flung in there some chairs
the web of a cough clawed

and I the prize-winner on the podium
and I the prize-winner on the podium

able to reach out and touch
the crumpled rind of your ear

to push through the velvets of dark
to lift
your black hair your blonde hair your tangled grey hair
to stroke
to take between finger and thumb
your lobe
to notice with peeled fingertip
this pucker that crease
this score
in front of your ear

Do you know it?
Does anyone know it?
Who has last touched you here?

To listen to the strong whisper of you
live in the dark, May-dust,
ten fingers lax on your clothes
ten toenails in your deep secrets of shoes
your furious beard-growth
your clicks

breasts' seep
the shrug of a mackintoshed vein
your flutings
your dampnesses

To say
Geese are leaving, breaking out of the bowl of sand, devastating
To say

I wanted to be Langston Hughes
to have written that poem about rivers
but I have known footpaths
I think I must know as much about sidewalks
as anyone in this world—
I don't know that I love them.

The sidewalk has held me in its rough broken arms—

You see the strangest things upon pavement
the most intimate turned about things
what should be inside a dog or a human—
money—
the puddle without a face—

To let
the square tip of the boot fall plumb on the line
or not
to break mother's back

A cracked American sidewalk
is not so different to anywhere else
Everything about the sidewalk is minor
No need to say secondary.

But after all it is you

And I have known childbirths
Blood rivers rising square and unflappable in cuboid hospital rooms
I have sluiced and hacked myself out over hospital rooms
I have poked out of closets holding caps for misshapen heads
I have zoomed down on myself
Na na naa na na

I've known childbirths
I've given birth to rivers

My body has bloodied impervious hospital rooms

Na na naa na na

My body has flowed like the rivers

Men cast their burnt fathers in me as I have given birth
I have ferried fever I have ferried my own death
in the charging yellow muck in the brown in the navy blue rushing N—
in my blood-red leaf-clad rivers

Na naa na na naa na na NANA
My blood has tumbled out in rivers.

We all have known childhoods
uncrossable as Zeno's worst fears
We all have heard the roar of the childhood shell clapped to the ear
Na-na-na-na-na

And I will tell you a story

> *—Step on a crack*
> *Break your mother's back*

About Johnny McGory

— Step on a line
Break your mother's spine

Will I begin it?

—Step in a hole
Break your mother's sugar bowl

That's all that's in it.

Still I will touch your eyelash
with my tiny comb.

from *Tympanum* (works-in-progress)

fwee chevy outsa

fwee shoey outsa
shall b'ug garridjj
imask muh ghueena
air il-lawn mara;
eh shool cush clodda
modjin iss traw knowna
o loo-un
guh sahrun
here ig balyev.

fwee shivee outsa
shall b'ug garridj
imask mo ghueena;
o craaaw cree
o woortch agna
o wegness guick
och ann tronn toch
here ig baljiv

querrida wirra *[sigh]*

on **ole** ditcha wirra *[exasperated]*
caw rock imm **leena** ↑
egg ear-a faskah leh duh lanav <u>nay</u>ofa—

craw will gock / **durr**iss / **doon**ta in air-ghun ↑
egg foo-ur iss oover on kinneh deign-a

[dark]   joe neh glocka leh kirra winsha
guh hillawn **mara**_san nyeer-her heenduh
egg keenga gjalla
nack fin-yeo-igga lasta
iss tinna vone-ah air halloch ine-ta

<u>keev</u>ney keen   *[exhale through nose]*

mwairra nah geevna
fohs ih mwagna⁓
bawneeny **bawn**a is leiynta gjala
leiynta gurumma? iss feshtee glossa   *[debonair]*
treouser iss drawirr ⁓*ll* deh vreideen walla

[darker]   avee-ock air-ara cawsucka ee-usta
egg three-ell air a naffrin madjin doughna
deh hewell **cuss**-air-ash der odda
a **woosglee camogiss** smuintya lomsa
air a **ghlinna** air *uir-yeh*
iss fohs air ah **van ached-t**

[very dark]   muara nah <u>geev</u>na <u>fohs</u> im miagna
coatee core-ree-a fadda darigga
coatee gurumeh leh *plureen* ↓ dahcha⁓
shawlta trow-in niece oss gallya
ah vee-ock air a genaw kyup/een/ee/okta
eh three-ell air ah na**frunn**⁓
marra gaina   *[gravelly]*

[priestly /   iss kay guh willud tig imackt oss <u>fash</u>ion ↓
recuperation] muara na geevna fohs im magna   *[resigned]*
iss mairya kinntcha
guh djai may dalla   *[resigned]*

151

shuhDAWN / fwee / oo-ig-niss   [sigh]
oo-igg-niss erin ill-aw-inn   [clipped]
nah-min**naw**-ah-vegg imm**aktt** ↑
oggus / nah / **firr**
in / a / go-knee inna nay-nor
 ↑ wickey / emmy-ockh / mwureeney mora inntum
pegeen misha / aveh irey sue us

derra ill-awn

          through aveh firrum leonaroo wegness
[dark]   *gonnock keyon sah chackiss doo-ech-kiss*
          cummus gock firr
          idull khun foo-era⁓
          oh glock on key-un
          mar **khay**la sue-inn ·

          maw **ubb**urch arminaw darr noolock   [wry]
          maw hague-ert chrey→
          chluckh gock *do*-egg-us   [woo!]
          dar vool dumb moirocka *hoorga*
          on layer ah knee cjart
          imma hooirim   [definitive]

          muh ubbert **foe**ss
          duh shmokta ginawisshh
          maw ailey **glow**→ oh huggar coy
          on near areesht
          knee core daw war ↓
          knee packa go *bwirrim* haw   [definitive]

[breath] taw on seal caydra ih njok awtchh
          imma gum**mah** gock claw
          firr // iss on key-un
          egg **cay**de-luh / deh gi**naw**
          ah hoor ongolua / a waws

oh mos to john millington synge

on **tuishk** / a **hug** too kun muh ghueena
own **gain vay** / done khorrie ghorriv
fwih kayla lay on chréy vyeo
iss on led iss gay / os lay-un iss domidj

near ayshtis / shkay-ull nuh gluck
vee-okta shkay-ull on talla
near spaysh lyat lyack nah kill
knee **hig** ayov as on ghrey warav

[breath] duh ghinna **dare**-drah rote-sa **road**
iss **cur**rock **knee**sha deh koss cann garriv
[low] jimmy dare drah iss kneesha **low**
iss kah pegeen leh shawneen ah-**hish** *[final]*

on lao-ur bugganaw iduh go-itch
os or kirrish / vair-eh air mwarin
love dare-druh knoisha / is pegeen **clo**
iss hug lame ghoshka jenna lyanney

taw khlakt muh gheena im**mah**
knee cower fast on ton marolla
ack guh dagga kyle coo-in
guh hinnish mjawin
bay na **brera** cnoo-sah eesh traw
air marring foess
ih djanga akt tring

PROVIDENCE SONG

Joseph Cacchia
Malcolm Starr,
Jason Chica
Adam Root,
T. Medeiros
Patrick Orr,
Gordon Klegraf
Byron Foote,
T. Schmidt
D. Teer
Herbert Single,
R. Turchetta
Kirk P. Stingle,
Al Fine
Pat Wynne
Sarah Vasquez
Ashwani Myne.

F. Dow
B. Ise
Chun Tu
A. Seitz,
Dina Vincent
C. Tucci,
I. Tejada
Diane Knights,
D.M. Snow
Mike Ayers
Jim Dee,
Yao, Huan
Pablo Torres,
Will Tilley,
R Straight
Juan Diaz
Delma Valdez,

Ann Zweir
Lois Ware
Linda Woodhams
Susan Fair.

Aj Daou
Ching Chuen Wong
C. Minot,
Douglas Pilger
Peter Sweet,
Jeff Dugas
I. Wood
Zack Gold,
Jon Ash
Ann Dore
Sameth Meas,
Zelia Trueb,
William Messa,
A. Glass,
Thelma Wright
George Lessard.
Ed Sheehan
Tim Behan
George, Erickson
Jesus, Ortiz.

NUNC LENTO SONITU

Joe Mann
Hilda Nilan,
N. Trice
Jordan Sheff;
Evelyn Mann
Tricia Pease
Ana Contreras,
A. Paz
Robert Maine.

F. Acosta
B. Washington
Gangshan Shi,
E. Reposa
D. Lessa,
J. L. Asquino
Cincinati Ware
S. R. Asquino
M. Anaya
D. Frenze
R. Dion
Lois Ware:

Donna Mangiante
D. Minicucci,
B. Cox
E. Amirhom
G. Manko,
M. D'Ercole
Chithy Saing
T. Keough
Dev Hoon
Mum Thoeun;
Leng Thoeung
J. Dee.

from *Lucky* (2011)

THE CENTIPEDE + THE LAPTOP

While the laptop is bone white or creamy white or luminous white or blue-white, it is hard to tell what color the centipede is; it is both transparent and really there.

The centipede is long, almost impossibly long, both flat and round, obviously capable of going in any direction at once. The laptop is quite sedate by comparison, slightly oblong, occupying space neatly and tactfully, withholding its giant secret of connectivity.

The centipede is dead. Or could be dead. Until it moves.

The laptop comes to life, like a woman, on a finger-stroke.

There is a space between them but they occupy the same plane. The laptop has the character of a platform, the centipede more that of the feather.

THE CENTIPEDE IN MY MIND'S EYE

The centipede in my mind's eye is a centipede no question but just that. It is a centipede delivered in one punch so to speak, without detail. If I zoom in on the centipede in my mind's eye, the image disintegrates. There are not enough pixels.

The centipede in real life provokes instant motion of the whirling windmill alarm blaring kind (were motion sound), whereas the image of a centipede, whether print or digital, is conducive to sustained looking by virtue of the removal from the scene of flailing limbs, whether human or centipedal.

From the tiled surface of the page, phrases such as "exclusively predatory taxon," "poison claw," "egg tooth," "organs of Tömösvary," "matriphagic," "many species lack eyes," "always have an odd number of legs," "in extreme cases the last pair of legs may be twice the length of the first pair," "face backwards"; and intimations such as "5,000 undescribed species" and "cryptic lifestyle" can be gathered and assessed with an attention impossible in live encounters between domesticated *homo sapiens* and *scutigera coleoptrata*, for example, whatever about cats.

Just as the great lump of the human body is irradiated by the corner-of-the-eye conduit of the feathery centipede, the exquisite speed of one translated instantly into the bumbling panic of the other, the former torpor of the one is morphed into the arrest mid-scuttle of the other; so too does the mind's eye require only a vivid crumb to jump into brute life images to make flesh crawl. Consider the simple names "Feather tail centipede," "Blue ring centipede," "Stone centipede," "Earth centipede," "Galápagos centipede," "Peruvian giant orange leg centipede," "Giant Red-headed centipede," "Red-headed centipede," "Giant Sonoran centipede," "Vietnamese centipede," and our chum "House centipede."[1]

In that theatre, of course, images will never be precise and may concomitantly incur commotion involving both emotional and physical states. They are nevertheless efficient, with the economy of poetry, despite their minimalism and blur.

---

[1]And are those quotation marks or legs?

FLOODLIGHTS

If you have an old house and it's not up to par with the houses of your friends and colleagues and you have been in it long enough to fix it up but you haven't fixed it up because you have no money or aren't able or just didn't get round to it yet but can't use the excuse of having just moved in anymore because you're in the house seven years and people don't invite you to dinner anymore because you never invite them back and anyway you feel bashful about accepting an invitation for the 4th or 5th time and want to, you know, start inviting people round yourself but don't want to expose the shortcomings of your living situation I have the solution for you: *Floodlights!* You can rent them fairly cheap or even invest in a set of your own if you intend to have a lot of dinner parties. You have to have high ceilings of course—did I mention I have an old house? Once installed you just blast that dinner table with 5,000 lumens and believe me, no one's going to be commenting on the state of your house. It's like that Edgar Allen Poe story "The Purloined Letter": *You blind with light.* The trick is, of course, to rein it in. You have to control the projection. You want the dining room ablaze but everything outside that shining space sheathed in velvety dark. You do not want the dust bunnies in the corner of the living room—or in the corner of the living room of your neighbor across the street—to jump into horrifying relief. It's extremely atmospheric as you can imagine. Your guests will feel like film stars. And there are other benefits. It's not that you don't have furniture—*it's that you moved it to make room for the lights.* It's not that you don't have rugs—*it's that you didn't want them torn up by the great claw feet of the floods so you rolled them away.* And if your guests do stumble out of the magic circle to go to the bathroom or explore the territory, their retinas will be too dazzled to see anything but whirling disks and orbs. They'll have to feel their way with their hands and when they return the food on their plate will look too real for words. Not only have you restored appetite to the realm of personal responsibility where it rightly belongs you have also more or less determined the topic of conversation for the evening, that is if people can bear to look each other in the eye long enough to talk. You can also rent searchlights with high-intensity beams each one of which has over six hundred million candlepower so your guests can easily find your house without GPS or *Mapquest*—the good old-fashioned way.

HATQUEST

I don't have a GPS but I do have state-of-the-art millinery so to speak in the shape of *Hatquest* (the extra-cranial positioning system). It looks very like a brain—worn on the outside of course. Other visual analogies might be: Marie-Antoinette's wig (when her head was still attached to her body) though not so large and tall and white. Also Marge Simpson's updo but not blue. Or an organic map. Yes, this one's good. Imagine you spread out your map. Not your ordinary anonymous/sterile/impersonal map but a map of the exact streets you will travel, your precise route, with a little red star for your starting point, your home, your north star, your Alpha and Omega, and another for your destination, your excursion, your beta, your B. Then you put *Peel-A-Way* all over your map, or something that turns it into pulp. And you scoop all that up like a jelly, the bright veins of your route glistening through, and it somehow accumulates shape and you pile it on top of your head. The little red stars are like barrettes, cunningly positioned. It beats all odds. It's also like an old-fashioned hairdryer in the beauty parlor, the kind you insert your head into. Also like a turban, printed of course. Also like those squidgy pipings of wet sand (themselves like renegade caulk from a whole-wheat gun) which lugworms, compact under the compact sand, throw out. Anyway, rather than attending to a pleasant though authoritative voice, you insert your head into this pellucid wobbly confection, also strangely comforting. Like a warm diaper but I digress. There is so much brain on the outside that one might be forgiven for thinking that the space within is empty. But no. There is a driver within. The analogy might be *streets* are to *Hatquest* as *car* is to *body* and *driver* is to *brain*. Still, obviously the brain has limits, the very limits that drove the driver to the purchase of *Hatquest* to begin with. If true purchase can ever be had on such a glittering slippery thing.

LUCKY

I'm not exactly a lucky person but I feel I may be lucky. I mean I never have been actually very lucky but I'm lucky in that I'm not very unlucky either. At least not *very* unlucky. Like I might be inclined to buy something the week before the price is halved or get my house insulated the year before the tax-break or buy the house at the height of the market just before it crashed but I'm not *unlucky*. I'm actually quite lucky. Not that I ever win raffles or lotteries, not lucky like that. Or not lucky like being in the right place at the right time or having fortuitous accidents or lucky breaks. I'm not the sort of person fortune smiles on exactly. If I were going up a hill and Fortune were coming down I'd probably glance over. Fortune might be busy or preoccupied but I'd certainly glance over I think. There are different kinds of lucky. Like I think if I did meet Fortune coming down the hill when I was going up I'd know it was Fortune like I wouldn't just trudge by. I'd probably stop and look after it a while. I'd probably think about it all for quite a while, even when I got to Whole Foods or wherever I was going up the hill to go. I wouldn't just blow it off or worse: not recognize it was Fortune in the first place. I'm lucky in that way. I know Fortune when I see it I think.

A HEAP OF SNOW

Driving out of Metro Honda in my Honda Civic I notice snow heaped in the back of the red pick-up truck in front driving out of Metro Honda before me between heaps of snow. I know it is a red pick-up because I know how this particular red drops its edges—glows—when paired with a sheet of even blue such as seen in the overarching sky like this sky arching over us as we drive to drive off the lot is this precise blue an overarching sheet of it held down at the invisible corners of the horizon as if with pins. *Who would shovel snow into a pick-up?* I say to my daughter. I mean *Look at all this snow.* We imagine a man in a padded jacket shoveling snow into the pick-up. A bearded man. Fresh from breakfast. I can't quite see his house from here, it's at my back, but I see the steam rising from him as he works and almost the warm kitchen with the steaming babies maybe one sticky hand opening and shutting toward the door as it shuts and a wife wiping back her hair with the back of a wet hand drawn from the soapy water of the steaming sink below. Then it hits us: *The sky did it!* Mike didn't shovel the snow! He just found it there. Dumped by the sky. And he didn't shovel it out. He's kind of lazy Mike. Maybe he lives alone. Or his marriage is only *so-so.* And this was a sort of double not-shovel, except one non-shovel was more scintilla than the other, if *scintilla* is a substantial enough word for the difference between the strange thing and the ordinary thing Mike didn't do. So, waiting to turn, we turn to consider, starry-eyed, the heap of snow in the back of the pick-up in front. The sky had done an adequate job, no question, But it was a standard heap. That's why I thought it had been shoveled in. It was not complete like a pyramid for example. *And they were made by men!* If the sky builds, you think, it will be something phenomenal. But then what the sky actually did was release the snow. The heap was the result of millions of snowflakes and the physics of how they pile and bond and build. That the result was similar to what a man or woman would produce with shoveling is a testament to the impartiality of physics. The heap produced by shoveling is incremental too, though in spade weights not flakes. The pyramids, in relation to building block and result, are closer to the sky, as they are literally. What the sky does with the snow in the back of the truck is as if a human did it. What the humans did with the pyramids is as if a mind like the sky dreamt it. But the physics is the same, unpreoccupied with culture. I understood all of this a lot better weeks later when I saw in the parking lot of a bank at night two snowplows working, the smaller one shoveling out the high frozen banks of snow and dumping it on the lot like food for a dog and the other, larger, plow scraping it up and cranking it into the container of a colossal truck drawn nearby, patient as a mother or anything on which smaller things feed.

Notes

State House Calendar

The Rhode Island State House in Providence is a magnificent & totally unlikely building, beached on Smith Hill under huge skies. I see it every day when I drive from my home in Mount Pleasant to the East Side of Providence where I work. For 13 months in 2004-2005, I recorded my first glimpse of it every morning: the color of the stone against the color of the sky. At the end of each month, these daily notes became a poem.

It was a time when I had no time—a way of snatching poetry where I could. I made the notes while driving; sometimes my daughters wrote them down. Rounding the corner from Chalkstone to Smith was a moment of great attention for us. One morning we hit Smith and— *no State House!* It was obliterated by fog.

Even though I was intent on color, it's worth mentioning that I always wore sunglasses. I tried to take a photo of the State House afterwards & was amazed how tangled up in telephone wires & traffic it was. I was able to handle light better with words than with a camera.

These poems are by no means the Rhode Island State House's only claim to fame—it is the fourth-largest self-supporting marble dome in the world. Also, it has an 11' tall gold-covered Independent Man on the top.

The brackets signify a second observation on any given day. July is short because I went away.

from *An Educated Heart*

"Baghdad," "Trapped," Rubble," and "Metaphor, Similes" are collage poems, assembled from phrases copied and pasted from Internet coverage of the invasion of Iraq, March/April 2003. "Almost" amends headlines from http://att.net. "Choose Your Husband" is also from the same source. The translations which comprise "An Educated Heart" were contributed by members of the Providence and Rhode Island School of Design communities.

from *Nelson & the Huruburu Bird*

"The Pillar" was a Dublin landmark for more than a hundred years. Erected in 1809 to commemorate British naval hero Horatio Nelson, the Pillar was blown up by the Irish Republican Army on Easter Monday, 1966, when Ireland was celebrating the fiftieth anniversary of the Easter Rising. The Irish phrases included in the poem are well-worn and colloquial: *dubh le daoine*, black with people/crowded; *ag baint dhá thaobh den bóthar*, taking both sides of the road/drunk; *íseal*, lowly; *uasal*, gentleman, noble. The reference here is to the inscription on the statue of the labor leader Jim Larkin, located close to where Nelson Pillar once stood at the center of Dublin: *Ní uasal bheith uasal / Ach sinn a bheith íseal. / Éirimís* (The great are only great because we are on our knees. Let us rise up); *póca of mo chóta*, pocket of my coat; *An Gúm*, government bookstore; *nua-Ghaeilge*, new Irish (anglicized spelling introduced in 1960s); *Ní bheidh . . . ár leithéid* refers to the phrase *Ní bheidh a leithéid ann arís*, a traditional formula for closing a story which means "His/her/their likes will never be seen again."

"Ordnungs" refers to Alan Dugan's "Answer to the Rilke Question," which in turn refers to the opening lines of Rilke's First Elegy: *Wer, wenn ich schriee, hörte mich denn aus der Engel / Ordnungen?* / "Who, if I cried, would hear me out of the Angel Orders?" Dugan's poem also refers to Berryman's Dream Song 3, line 13: "Rilke was a *jerk*.

In "Early Morning, Dublin," *remembering only the murdered and disgraced* refers to Dolores Lynch and Lynn Madden, activists for the legalization of prostitution in Dublin, with whom I worked as a journalist in the 1980s. Dolores Lynch, and her aunt, were murdered by John Cullen, a pimp.

"Grooming": The story of Oisín and *Tír na nÓg* (Land of Youth) is well known in Ireland; Niamh of the Golden Hair lured Oisín away. He asked to return to Ireland for a visit; Niamh agreed, warning him not to dismount from her white steed. He fell, or bent down from the horse, touched the ground and immediately all the years he had missed descended on him, and he died. *Beann Éadair*, or Howth, is a promontory on the north side of Dublin Bay, said to be the profile of Oisín's father Finn McCool, where he fell into the sea.

"A Salute to the Cape Verdean Community in Boston": I found these comments in the visitors' book for an exhibition of photographs of Cape Verde, and the Cape Verdean community in Boston, by Beverley Conley, Boston Public Library, 1994. I come from a deep tradition of emigration. At that time, as it happens, I was tramping around Boston for a week in the snow, staying in the YWCA, to keep my U.S. visa open though I was a student and single parent in Ireland. Shortly afterwards, I emigrated, with my child.

"Directions for The Dead" was taken from John Huston's film script for *The Dead.*

from *Tympanum*

This work-in-progress comprises a constellation of investigations of sound in poetry, reclaiming for the living tongue and ear the rhythms and textures of languages and literatures proximate, but almost beyond ken, for the purpose of claiming what is, adulterated though it may be, and expanding vocal range in contemporary poetry. Works-in-progress include:

har sawlya: A work-in-progress focusing on sound in the poems of the mid-20th century Irish language poet Máirtín Ó Díreáin, who was born in Irish-speaking Inis Mór, the largest of the very small Aran Islands, though he wrote his poetry in English-speaking Dublin where he worked as a civil servant throughout his adult life. The title, *Har Sawlya*, is a phonetic rendering of a common Irish phrase meaning *across the sea / abroad / beyond / emigrated / gone.* I strive to render phonetically, in illuminated print, the sounds of Ó Díreáin's poetry as I hear them on the audio CD *Máirtín Ó Díreáin Dánta—á léamh ag an bhfile* (Gael Linn 2010). I then make an audio recording of each poem, based on my transcription, essentially making a "cover" of Ó Díreáin's voice. When I have recorded all 30 tracks, I hope to isolate a set of distinctive sounds which I find particularly difficult to say, and to compose with those. I may also compose with the sighs and heaves with which Ó Díreáin punctuates his reading, i.e., I may work with his breath.

songs + meditations: A poetry + poetics project consisting of a set of poems made from harnessing the rhythms of John Donne's poems and sermons to names from the Providence phonebook, followed by a set of prose meditations on color in contemporary poetics. In *Songs*, each poem looks like a list of names reflective of the diverse population of a medium-sized American city, but sounds like the poems and sermons of John Donne. Metaphysical poetry or the phonebook: which is more defunct?

Acknowledgments

I would like to thank most sincerely the editors of the following presses for their generosity in granting permission to reprint material. Editors are a poet's best readers and, in the poetry world, are invariably poets themselves:

Randolph Healy, Wild Honey Press, for *Nelson & the Huruburu Bird* (2003), also *The Pillar* (2000) and *Vivas* (2005).

Jane Sprague, Palm Press, for *An Educated Heart* (2005).

Belladonna* Collective, for *Kalends* (2005).

Kenneth Goldsmith, /ubu Editions, for *SOS Poetry* (2007).

Keith Tuma, Miami University Press, for *Talk Poetry* (2007).

Susana Gardner and Arielle Greenberg-Bywater, Dusie Kollektiv, for *State House Calendar* (2009).

Adam Robinson, Publishing Genius Press, for *The Best of (What's Left of)* Heaven (2010).

Dawn Pendergast, Little Red Leaves Textile Series, for *Lucky* (2011).

I would also like to thank all the editors who first published the poems collected in these books and this volume; also Jodi Chilson for her continued interest in the poems from *Har Sawlya*, included in the *Tympanum* section here; and Dirceu Villa for his long-standing engagement as a translator, editor, and publisher of my work in Brazil.

I would like to express deep gratitude to the entire editorial and design team at Barrow Street Press; you have honored my work with your passionate interest, commitment, expertise, and care.

Thank you, John O'Regan, of Gandon Editions, for permission to reprint details from *Profile 27—Michael Cullen* (Gandon Editions 2007), and for supplying digital images.

Thank you, Michael Cullen, for permission to include details of your paintings "Elephant in Blue" (2004) and "Dancer and Elephant" (2005) on the cover of this book. You have kept my spirit alive and revived, Michael, from Henrietta Street to Siberia, cheered by the peerless example of your vital self and work, and regardless of distance or the years, your genius for keeping in touch.

MAIRÉAD BYRNE is the author of poetry collections *The Best of (What's Left of)* Heaven, *Talk Poetry, SOS Poetry*, and *Nelson & the Huruburu Bird*; and poetry chapbooks including *State House Calendar, An Educated Heart, Vivas, Kalends* and *The Pillar*. Collaborations with visual artists include *Jennifer's Family* (photographs by Louisa Marie Summer), *Lucky* (illustrations by Abigail Lingford), and three books with Irish painters. Mairéad Byrne is the cofounder, curator and emcee for *couscous*, a poetry/music/performance series which has been running monthly for five years in Providence, where she is employed as Professor of Poetry + Poetics at Rhode Island School of Design.

Barrow Street Poetry

You Have To Laugh: New + Selected Poems
Mairéad Byrne (2013)

Wreck Me
Sally Ball (2013)

Blight, Blight, Blight, Ray of Hope
Frank Montesonti (2012)

Self-evident
Scott Hightower (2012)

Emblem
Richard Hoffman (2011)

Mechanical Fireflies
Doug Ramspeck (2011)

Warranty in Zulu
Matthew Gavin Frank (2010)

Heterotopia
Lesley Wheeler (2010)

This Noisy Egg
Nicole Walker (2010)

Black Leapt In
Chris Forhan (2009)

Boy with Flowers
Ely Shipley (2008)

Gold Star Road
Richard Hoffman (2007)